Prayers and Thoughts from World Religions

PRAYERS AND THOUGHTS FROM WORLD RELIGIONS

SID G. HEDGES

Each sees one colour of thy rainbow-light;
Each looks upon one tint and calls it heaven;
Thou art the fullness of our partial sight;
We are not perfect till we find the seven;
Gather us in.

JOHN KNOX PRESS
Richmond, Virginia

First published as *With One Voice* by the Religious Education Press, Pergamon Press Ltd., Oxford, 1970

American edition published by John Knox Press, Richmond, Virginia, 1972

Library of Congress Cataloging in Publication Data

Hedges, Sidney George, 1897-
    Prayers and thoughts from world religions.

    First published in 1970 under title: With one voice.
    1. Prayers. 2. Meditations. I. Title.
[BL560.H4 1972]   200   72-1875
ISBN 0-8042-2500-1

As children, many of us learned the colours of the rainbow from the initial letters

ROYGBIV

(Red, Orange, Yellow, Green, Blue, Indigo, Violet)

The initial letters of each theme-subject follow the sequence of this mnemonic, with the addition of W for White.

PREFACE

I HAVE knelt with eyes open in a Catholic church; I have sat upright with closed eyes in a Quaker meeting house; I have put on my hat and stood in a synagogue; I have taken off my shoes and prostrated myself in a mosque; I have even tried—rather unsuccessfully—to sit cross-legged with Buddhists. In each instance we were praying. The modes were different, the aim and the achievement was the same. The familiar Old Testament phrase perhaps best expresses it: 'Be still, and know that I am God'.

A Burmese friend once told me: 'From 5 to 6 a.m. each day I meditate. Without time for being still my life would go to pieces'.

In every age, in every land, people have felt such need, and in prayer and meditation have sought Truth and God. An understanding and appreciation of such searchings as are expressed in other faiths does not mean for the Christian, for example, any lessening of his own loyalty and belief in the sublime revelation of Jesus. Rather it increases his own spiritual awareness by showing fresh and unsuspected colours in God's 'rainbow light'.

It has been my aim in this book to bring together flashes of illumination and colour from different and divergent sources, revealing how, when followers of any great living faith reach out in sincerity, true religious experience results. There is a unity in the diversity; a common ground on which the world's varied peoples can become aware of belonging to 'one family under God'. All speak with one voice.

Confucius said: 'If you have two loaves sell one and buy a lily'. We have from Jesus: 'Consider the lilies . . . .' Buddha, as his disciples one day sat round him awaiting his teaching, said nothing, but held up a lotus flower. His nearest and dearest disciple, Ananda, at length broke the silence: 'Master, I understand!' Confucius, Jesus, Buddha; all similarly could find eternal truth in a flower.

So here are multicoloured prayers, sayings, themes for meditation— Bahai, Buddhist, Christian, Confucian, Egyptian, Hindu, Jain, Jewish, Muslim, Shinto, Sikh, Stoic, Sufi, Taoist, Zoroastrian.

To teenagers at a school assembly they can bring that freshness which stimulates real participation and helps to dispel the frequent suspicion in a questing mind that religion is always dogmatic and intolerant. To their seniors, staled by the familiar and almost unaware of other traditions, personal religion may be helped to new life, and current ecumenical yearnings jumped imaginatively forward into concern for world inter-faith communion.

Deity pronouns have been printed capitals or lower-case as in the original sources. Under each item, people's names are in capital letters; book-titles are in italics.

My sincere thanks are especially due to the following who have checked over and advised on particular sections of this book:

A. S. Chhatwal, Secretary of Sikh Cultural Society of Great Britain.

David and Mrs. Jenkerson, Oxford Bahai Community.

The Venerable Kapilavaddho Bhikkhu, Dhammapadipa (Buddhist) Temple, London.

Dr. Ali M. Khan, Lecturer on Islam, Woking Mosque.

Bishnu Deo Narayan, President East London Hindu Centre.

Rabbi Roger Pavey, West Central Liberal Jewish Synagogue.

The Title Index at the back of the book can be used, combined with the sectional divisions, in finding particular themes or subjects. The Source Index gives information about people and names. The Faiths Index simply puts the numbered items into their respective groupings. The Appendix may intrigue some.

Bicester   S.G.H.

To my friends in the
WORLD CONGRESS OF FAITHS
who are seeking 'to promote a spirit of fellowship among
mankind through religion and to awaken and develop a world
loyalty'.

REVERENTIAL AWE

. . . who art in heaven, hallowed be Thy name . . .

1

THE RAINBOW PRAISETH THEE

The rainbow praiseth Thee, O Most High; very beautiful it is in the brightness thereof; it compasseth the heaven about with a glorious circle, and Thy hands have bended it.

The clear firmament, the beauty of heaven, the sun at his rising, declare Thy work. The moon to serve in her season, a light that decreaseth in her perfection; the glory of the stars giving light in the highest places, they stand in their order, O Holy One, and never faint in their watches.

By Thy commandment the snow falls apace, Thou sendeth the swift lightnings, the noise of the thunder maketh the earth to tremble. Thou, Lord, art terrible and very great and marvellous is Thy power.

There are yet hid greater things than these, for we have seen but a few of Thy works. For Thou, O Lord, hath made all things, and to the godly hath given wisdom.

Jewish   *Ecclesiasticus 43* (adapted)

2

DO NEVER PRAY

Do never pray;
But only say
—O Thou!

Christian   JAMES STEPHENS

3

THERE IS ONE GOD

There is One God,
He is the Supreme Truth,
He, the Creator, is without fear
And without hate.
He, the Omnipresent, pervades the Universe,
He is not born, nor does He die to be born again.
True in the beginning, true throughout the ages,
True even now, and forever shall be true.

Sikh   *Japji (Mool Mantra)*

4

GOD IS GREATER THAN ALL ELSE

God is greater than all else. Glory and praise to Thee, O God. Blessed is Thy Name, and exalted is Thy Majesty. There is no one worthy of worship and service but Thee.

God is greater than all else. Glory be to God, the Exalted. God accepts him who is grateful to Him. O our God, all praise be unto Thee. God is greater than all else.

Glory to my Lord, the most High. God is greater than all else.

Muslim

5

WE ALL WORSHIP

We all, verily, worship God.
We all, verily, bow down before God.
We all, verily, are devoted unto God.
We all, verily, give praise unto God.
We all, verily, yield thanks unto God.
There is none other God but Thee, the One, the Single,
    the Powerful, the Omniscient, the Bountiful.

Bahai   BAHA'U'LLAH

6

LIGHT TO THE EARTH

We praise you,
O Lord our God,
King of the universe,
Maker of light
and Creator of darkness,
Giver of peace
and Creator of all things.
In your mercy
you give light to the earth
and to all who dwell in it,

and in your goodness
you renew the work of creation
continually, day by day.
We praise you, O Lord,
Creator of Light.

Jewish   *Service of the Heart*

7

PROTECTOR OF THE POOR

There is one God, passionless, formless, uncreated, the universal soul,
the supreme spirit, the all-pervading, whose shadow is the world; who
has become incarnate and done many things, only for the love that he
bears to his faithful people; all-gracious and compassionate to the
humble; who in his mercy ever refrains from anger against those whom
he loves and knows to be his own, protector of the poor, all good, all
powerful, the lord.

Hindu   TULSI DAS

8

LORD OF LIGHT

The Creator, Lord of Light, praise we.
The Teacher, Lord of Purity, praise we.
The day-times praise we.
The pure water praise we.
The stars, the moon, the sun, the trees, praise we.
The mountains, the pastures, dwellings and fountains, praise we . . .
The well-created animals praise we.
We praise all good men; we praise all good women.
We praise thee, our dwelling-place, O Earth.
We praise thee, O God, Lord of the dwelling-place.

Zoroastrian   *Zend-Avesta*

9

THOU ONE GOD

O Thou One God, O Lord of Eternity, how excellent are Thy designs.
Thou didst create the earth according to Thy heart. Thou settest man
on his place and suppliest his need.

Egyptian   AKHNATON (probably)

10

TRUE PARENT OF ALL THINGS

Of old, in the beginning, there was the great chaos, without form and
dark. Thou, O Spiritual Sovereign, didst first divide the grosser parts
from the purer. Thou madest heaven; Thou madest earth; Thou madest
man. All things got their being with their reproducing power. Thou
didst produce the sun and moon and five planets, and pure and
beautiful was their light. It is thou alone, O Lord, who art the true
parent of all things.

Chinese

11

THE PRIMAL, THE PURE

Praise, praise to Thee, the primal, the pure. Thou hast no beginning;
Thou hast no end; Thou art the same in every age.

Sikh

12

THOU WHO HAST NO EQUAL

O Self-existent One
Who art beyond our comprehension,
O Thou omnipotent One
Who hast no equal in power and greatness,
Who art without a second:
O Thou merciful One
Who guidest stray souls to the right path,
Thou art truly our God.

Sufi   ABDULLAH ANSARI

13

A FIT AND HOLY NAME

O Lord of light, whose glory we feel amid the darkness of our thought, we would speak with thee in lowly prayer, but we cannot name thee with a fit and holy name. Where art thou, O thou living God, that we may join all wise and blessed souls in serving thee? Thou art too near for our eye to see thee, too far for our outstretched mind to reach; yet is thy presence even in our midst; and along the pathway of our life, and the wanderings of our hearts, and the transit of our days, we are alone unchangeably with thee.

Christian   JAMES MARTINEAU

14

THE MARVELLOUS MAGICIAN

O Lord, eternal Teacher, Thou whom we can neither name nor understand, but who we would realise more and more at every moment, enlighten the intelligence, illumine our hearts, transfigure the consciousness; may everybody awaken to the true life, escape from egoism and its train of sorrow and anguish, in order to take refuge in Thy divine and pure Love, source of all peace and all happiness. My heart so full of Thee seems to expand to infinity, and my intelligence wholly enlightened with Thy Presence shines like the purest diamond. Thou art the marvellous magician, he who transfigures everything, makes beauty emerge out of ugliness, light out of darkness, clear water out of mud, knowledge out of ignorance and kindness out of egoism.

In Thee, by Thee, for Thee we live and Thy law is the supreme master of our life.

May Thy will be done in every place, may Thy peace reign over the whole earth!

Hindu   SRI AUROBINDO

15

ADORATION

Praise giving . . . Lord of Truth . . .
Fair of face, who is on His great throne,
The One God . . . Beloved as King . . .

May He give life, prosperity and health,
Keenness, favour, and love,
And that mine eyes may behold Thee every day.

Egyptian   Hymn, *c*. 1300 B.C.

16

THE LAMP ON A PILLAR

God (Allah) is the light of the heavens and the earth;
The likeness of His light is as a pillar on which is a lamp.
The lamp is in a glass,
The glass as it were a glittering star
Kindled from a Blessed Tree,
an olive that is neither of the East nor of the West
whose oil well nigh would shine,
even if no fire touched it;
   Light upon Light;
God guides towards His Light whoever so desires.
And God sets forth parables for mankind.
   and God knows all things.

Muslim   *Koran 24*. 35

17

GOD, MY ALL IN ALL

Thou alone art the taste of my tongue,
Thou art my tongue, ears and eyes,
Thou art the soul within my body; Thou art my mind; Yea,
   Thou art my all in all.
Thou dwellest alone in my heart, and in my breath; Thou
   art the life within my body.
Thou fillest my whole body from head to foot;
Thou fillest my heart like water.
I have none but Thee. Thou alone art the life within me.

Hindu   DADU

18

HIM WHO IS THE UNCREATED

Lauded be Thy name, O my God! I testify that no thought of Thee, howsoever wondrous, can ever ascend into the heaven of Thy knowledge, and no praise of Thee, no matter how transcendent, can soar up to the atmosphere of Thy wisdom. From eternity Thou hast been removed far above the reach and the ken of the comprehension of Thy servants, and immeasurably exalted above the strivings of Thy bondslaves to express Thy mystery. What power can the shadowy creature claim to possess when face to face with Him who is the Uncreated?

Powerful art Thou to do what pleaseth Thee. Thou, truly, art the All-Glorious, the All-Wise.

Bahai   BAHA'U'LLAH

19

O LORD, CREATOR

We worship Thee O Lord. Thou hast created us and those before us. Thou hast appointed the earth a resting place for us, the sky a canopy, causing water to pour down from the heavens, thereby producing fruits as food for us. There is no God but Thee.

Muslim

20

THE SOURCE OF LIGHT

I believe Thee to be the best being of all, the source of light for the world. Every one shall choose Thee as the source of light, O most beneficent spirit, Divine Being. For Thou, O Lord, shall be unto us as the everlasting light.

Zoroastrian   *Zend-Avesta*

21

LIFE OF WORLDS

O God, mysterious and infinite, thou art the first and thou art the last. As our weeks pass away and our age rises or declines, we still return to thee who art the same. We seek thee as the sole abiding light amid the shadows of perishable things. O thou most ancient God, to whom the heavens are but of yesterday, and the life of worlds but as the shooting star, there is no number of thy days and mercies, and what can we do, O Lord, but throw ourselves on thee who failest not, and from whom our pathway is not hid. With solemn and open heart we would meet thee here.

Christian   JAMES MARTINEAU

22

IN THE BEGINNING

In the beginning Thou didst exist O God, the Cause of the elements, the One Lord of the Universe upholding this earth and the heaven. To Thee we offer our prayer.

Hindu   *Rig Veda*

23

WITHOUT THE DIN OF WORDS

O Thou, who fillest heaven and earth, ever acting, ever at rest, who art everywhere and everywhere art wholly present, who art not absent even when far off, who with Thy whole being fillest yet transcendest all things, who teachest the hearts of the faithful without the din of words; teach us, we pray Thee.

Christian   ST. AUGUSTINE

24

GOD WHO ALWAYS EXISTS

In the name of God the Beneficent, the Forgiver, the Kind. May there be praise for the name of God, who has always existed, exists, and will always exist. Thou art the Lord, great, mighty, wise, creator, nourisher, protector, supporter, righteous forgiver, dispenser of good justice, all powerful.

Zoroastrian

25

GOD THE EVERLIVING

God! There is no Deity but He, the Everliving, the Self-subsisting by whom all subsist. Slumber overtakes Him not, nor sleep. To Him belongs whatever is in the heavens and whatever is in the earth. Who is he that can intercede with Him but by His permission? He knows what is before them and what is behind them, and they encompass nothing of His knowledge except when He pleases. His throne extends over the heavens and the earth, and the preserving of them tires Him not, and He is the Most High, the Great.

Muslim *Koran 2. 255*

26

THE DIVINE HERDSMAN

He is a forgiving God; kind to the distressed,
Responsive to love, and merciful always.
The Divine Herdsman places Himself at the head of His straying
    flock,
And feeds them, one and all.
He is the Primal Being, the Cause of all causes, the Creator,
The very breath of life to those who love Him.
Whoever worships Him is cleansed.
And is attached to love and devotion.
We are low, ignorant and devoid of virtue,
But we have come to Thy protection, O Lord of all resources.

Sikh GURU ARJAN

27

AUTHOR OF ALL BEING

Thee Author of all being,
Fountain of light, Thyself invisible —
Amidst the glorious brightness where Thou sit'st

Thron'd inaccessible, but when Thou shad'st
The full blaze of Thy beams, and through a cloud
Drawn round about Thee like a radiant shrine
Dark with excessive bright Thy skirts appear,
Yet dazzle Heav'n.

Christian   JOHN MILTON

28

WONDER

O Lord! Increase my astonishment in Thee!

Bahai

29

THE SAME GOD FOR EVER

Thou art one and the same God, pleased and displeased by the same
things for ever.

Zoroastrian

30

GOD IS SUPREME

*Alláhu Akbar, Alláhu Akbar. Lá iláha ill-Alláh. Wa'lláhu Akbar, Alláhu
Akbar wa lilláhil-hamd.*

God is Supreme, God is Supreme. There is no God except God. And
God is Supreme, God is Supreme and all praise is due to Him.

Muslim

31

OUR HEARTS TURN LONGINGLY

From man's unfaithfulness
Our hearts turn longingly to Thee,
O Love eternal and unchanging.

From man's weak fickleness
Our hearts turn longingly to Thee
O Will immutable.

From man's small vapourings
Our hearts turn longingly to Thee,
O Word unspeakable.

From man's most sordid meanness
Our hearts turn longingly to Thee,
O Giver without stint or limit.

From man's exceeding feebleness
Our hearts turn longingly to Thee,
O Might omnipotent.

From man's gross filth
Our hearts turn longingly to Thee,
O Purity divine and absolute.

From man's deformity
Our hearts turn longingly to Thee,
O Beauty perfect and ineffable.

Christian   JOHN S. HOYLAND

32

GOD IN HIS GREATNESS

Who indeed is it with grace in his tones,
Who sends his smile out to the dwellings of the suffering,
Who shows his compassion on life and is victor?
Yes, it is God himself, who sits on the throne,
With power over sin, over grief, over death.
None other is like to our God in his greatness.

Egyptian   Poem *c*. 400 B.C.

33

THE ETERNAL OM*

God created the universe, like a musical instrument and filled it with His word as its sounds. God created the eternal OM out of Himself.

Hindu   DADU

(*OM, pronounced "ome" or "oom", is considered to have sacred significance as being a basic formulation of universal energy from which sound and speech have evolved. Sometimes translated "peace". (See 284, 403.)

34

FATHER AND MOTHER TO MAN

Thou art the Ocean of Mercy, the Friend of Man, the Friend of Sinners, the Bountiful, the Destroyer of Sorrow the Cherisher of the Poor, Thou art both Father and Mother to man.

Sikh

35

MAJESTIC GOD

O, under various sacred names adored!
Divinity supreme! All potent Lord!
Author of nature, whose unbounded sway
And legislative power all things obey.

Majestic God, all hail! To Thee belong
The suppliant prayer and tributary song:
To Thee from all Thy mortal offspring due:
From Thee we came, from Thee our being drew.

But, O Great Father, thunder-ruling God,
Who in thick darkness mak'st thy dread abode,
Thou, from whose bounty all good gifts descend,
Do Thou from ignorance mankind defend!
The clouds of vice and folly, O control
And shed the beams of wisdom on the soul!

Stoic   CLEANTHES

36

THE SHAPER, THE FASHIONER

He is God (Allah), the Creator, the Shaper out of naught, the Fashioner. His are the most beautiful names. All that is the heavens and the earth glorifieth Him_ and He is the Mighty, the Wise.

Muslim   *Koran 59. 24*

37

CLOSER IS HE ThAN BREATHING

You Lord are near, yet we climb a palm tree to see you.

Sikh   KABIR (adapted)

38

FAITH, AND DEAD THINGS

They tell us of systems and rites,
Of schemes of redemption, philosophies, dogmas and creeds:

But how can faith deal with dead things
In a world where are mountains and forests and stars,
Children's laughter and love, and the touch of God's hand?

Faith is vivid and living and warm,
Faith is friendship with Thee.

Not from books and authority, pedants or priests,
Cometh faith, but from life lived with Thee,
O Master divine,
From the joy of the friendship of God.

Christian   JOHN S. HOYLAND

39

THOU CHAMPION OF THE POOR MAN

Praise to Thee . . . My heart desireth to see Thee. My heart rejoices, O
Thou champion of the poor man. Thou art the father of the motherless,
the husband of the widow . . . Thy name is like the taste of life, it is
like the taste of bread to the child, a loincloth to the naked. Thou art
like the breath of freedom to one who has been in prison. Turn Thyself
to us O Lord of Eternity. Thou wast here ere we had come into
existence. Verily the worship of Thee is good. Turn away fear. Place joy
in the hearts of men. Joyful is the man that sees Thee.

Egyptian   Prayer to Amon 1300 B.C.

40

BEYOND OUR KNOWING

Who beholds me formulates it not, and who formulates me beholds me
not.

Muslim

41

EXALT YE THE LORD

Thine, O Lord, is the greatness, the power, the glory and the majesty;
for all that is in the heavens and in the earth is Thine. Thine, O Lord, is
the Kingdom, and Thou are exalted supreme above all. Exalt ye the
Lord our God and bow down to His footstool, for He is holy, Exalt ye
the Lord our God, and worship at His holy mount, for the Lord our
God is holy.

Jewish   *Prayer Book*

42

LIGHT OF ALL LIGHTS

God is the light of all lights and luminous beyond all the darkness of
our ignorance. He is knowledge and the object of knowledge.

Hindu   *Bhagavad Gita*

43

PURE WORSHIP

High and holy Lord God Almighty, who art the fountain of all true
thoughts and right resolves, be pleased to still the tumult of earthly
cares within our breasts, and fill our minds with deep devotion; that for
a little while we may rise above the jar and fret of daily life, and join
with grateful hearts in that pure worship, which from spirits higher and
holier than ours for ever ascends before thy throne.

Christian   W. GRAY ELMSLIE

44

VICISSITUDES OF LIFE

One Thou exaltest, and givest him dominion,
Another Thou castest as food to the fishes;
One Thou enrichest with treasure, like Karun,
Another Thou feedest with the bread of affliction;
Nor is that a proof of Thy love, nor this of Thy hatred;
For Thou, the Creator of the World, knowest what is fit;
Thou assignest to each man his high or low estate:
And how shall I describe Thee? THOU ART WHAT THOU ART!

Muslim   FERDUSI

45

HIS NAMES ARE MANY

God is hidden to gods and men,
No man has searched his similitude,
He is a secret to all his creatures;
No man knoweth a name by which to call Him . . .
His name is a secret to all his children,
His names are without number.

Ancient Egyptian

46

I BOW TO THEE

Obeisance to Thee O Lord,
Thou art the sun which dispels the darkness of ignorance,
Thou art free and massive consciousness,
Mercy is Thy form
And Thou art all good.
Thou art the support of the devotee
And the being of all that are.
Thou art the revelation of all revelations.
I bow to Thee as in front of me, as on either side of me,
As behind me, as below me, and as above me,
Grant me this, that Thou hast Thy abode ever in my mind.

Hindu   *Tantraraja Tantra*

47

A MILLION TONGUES

Though one had a million tongues,
Even then one would fail to recount God's praises!

Sikh   GURU GOBIND SINGH

48

A THOUSAND TONGUES

O for a thousand tongues to sing
My great Redeemer's praise!

Christian   CHARLES WESLEY

49

GOD, THE ALMIGHTY

Know that evil and good are from Him that hath no partner;
Whose operations have no beginning and no end.
When He says BE! it is done to his hand;
He Was, and ever Was; and Is, and ever Is.

Muslim   FERDUSI

50

ALL WORLDS

In Thee, Beloved, is light:
And the light doth shine
In darkness of the world.
And the world knows it not!
O Light! Eternal Light!
With a million eyes dost Thou
Fill all worlds, all stars and suns.
With a mercy immeasurable
Thou dost shine on me —
A pilgrim through endless space
To Thy Holy Shrine.

Hindu   MIRA

51

THE BEAUTY OF HOLINESS

Give unto the Lord, O ye mighty, give unto the Lord glory and strength.

Give unto the Lord the glory due unto his name; worship the Lord in the beauty of holiness.

Jewish   *Psalm 29*

52

IN ALL FULLNESS

Thou art goodness, all goodness, the greatest goodness. Thou art love, Thou art wisdom, Thou art humility, Thou art patience, Thou art security, Thou art riches in all fullness.

Christian   ST. FRANCIS

53

THOU MOST HIGH

I will praise Thee, O Lord, with my whole heart; I will shew forth all Thy marvellous works. I will be glad and rejoice in Thee; I will sing praise to Thy name, O Thou most High.

Jewish   *Psalm 9*

54

THOU GOD ALONE

Thou God alone art worthy of praise,
Thy Name is worthy of repetition,
Thy Thought is worthy of contemplation,
Thy Command is worthy of obedience,
Thy Majesty is worthy of service.

Muslim

55

ALL CONTEMPLATE THEE

The Arabs of Arabia,
The French of France,
The Kureshis of Kandhar,
Meditate on Thee.
The Marathas and the Maghda people,
The Dravidians and the Talinganians,
Concentrate their minds on Thee.
The Chinese and the Manchurians,
The Tibetans of Tibet,
All contemplate Thee.

Sikh   GURU GOBIND SINGH

56

THE ETERNAL ONE

God is the Eternal One, he is everlasting and is without end. He is
everlasting and eternal. He endureth for time without end, and he will
exist to all eternity.

Ancient Egyptian

57

IN EVERY PLACE

In every place where you find the imprint of men's feet there am I.

Jewish   *Talmud*

58

LET US MEDITATE

Let us meditate upon the adorable light of Thy Radiance; may it stimulate our intellect.

Hindu   *Rig Veda*

59

CREED OF MAIMONIDES

I believe with perfect faith that the Creator, blessed be his name, is the author and Guide of everything that has been created, and that he alone has made, does make, and will make all things.

I believe with perfect faith that the Creator, blessed be his name, is a Unity, and that there is no unity in any manner like unto his, and that he alone is our God, who was, is, and will be.

I believe with perfect faith that the Creator, blessed be his name, is not a body, and that he is free from all the accidents of matter, and that he has not any form whatsoever.

I believe with perfect faith that the Creator, blessed be his name, is the first and the last.

I believe with perfect faith that to the Creator, blessed be his name, and to him alone, it is right to pray, and that it is not right to pray to any besides him.

Jewish   Articles of a creed formulated by
MOSES MAIMONIDES

60

BRIGHTLY SHINING ONE

Sing praise to Him the Lord of Light. Son of Strength, blessed brightly shining One, whose light is excellent. May we by Thine own fires be well supplied with fire, O Son of Strength, O Lord of Might. Give us the splendour Lord, who art most prompt with sacred gifts, and who adore the Perfect God.

Hindu   *Rig Veda*

61

ADORATION AND PRAISE

Hail! For lawful it is that all mortals should address
    Thee
For we are thy offspring . . .
Therefore will I hymn Thee, and sing Thy might forever.
For Thee doth all this universe that circles round the
    earth obey, moving whithersoever Thou leadest, and is
    gladly swayed by Thee . . .
Naught is done on the earth without Thee, O God,
    nor in the divine sphere of the heavens, nor in the sea,
Save the works that evil men do in their folly.

Stoic   CLEANTHES' *Hymn to Zeus*

62

HEAT AND DUST OF THE TOWN

Father, we thank thee that, just as in the heat and dust of the town we may remember the coolness and cleanness, the silence and peace, of the country, which lieth all around us unseen, with its birds and flowers, woods and streams—so in the turmoil of our hurrying lives, in the midst even of pain and failure, we may remember that beyond and all around is thyself, quiet and cool, trusty, beautiful and brave, in whom is our hope and our stay for ever.

Christian   Indian College Prayers

63

THROUGHOUT ALL GENERATIONS

I will extol Thee, my God, O King; and I will bless Thy Name for ever and ever. Every day will I bless Thee; and I will praise Thy name for ever and ever. I will speak of the glorious honour of Thy majesty, and of Thy wondrous works. All Thy works shall praise Thee, O Lord; and Thy saints shall bless Thee. They shall speak of the glory of Thy Kingdom and talk of Thy power; To make known to the sons of men his mighty acts, and the glorious majesty of his kingdom. Thy kingdom is an everlasting Kingdom, and Thy dominion endureth throughout all generations.

Jewish   *Psalm 145*

OTHERS

. . . as we forgive those who trespass against us . . .

64

THE GOLDEN RULE

a

Do unto others as you would they should do unto you.

Christian   JESUS

b

Do nothing unto others which you would not have done unto yourself.

Buddhist   from scriptures

c

May we take the word of reciprocity to serve as our rule of life—what we do not wish others to do to us, may we not do unto them.

Confucian

d

Do unto all men as you would wish to have done unto you.

Muslim   MUHAMMAD

e

O God!
May I treat others
As I would be treated
What I like not for myself
May I dispense not to others.

Sufi   ABDULLAH ANSARI

f

Do not approve for another what you do not like for yourself.

Zoroastrian   *Gospel of Zarathushtra*

g

Do not do unto others that which you would not have them do unto you.

Jewish   HILLEL

65

LOVE AND HATE

Return love for hatred.

Taoist   *Tao-Te-Ching 79*

66

RULES OF THE GOOD LIFE

He alone will obtain an excellent end
Who does good to others, and knows not how to reproach them,
Who is merciful to all creatures, and cherishes cattle;
And in the desert gives water to the thirsty:
Who is calm and never blames any.

Hindu   TUKARAMA

67

WELL SPOKEN OF

If you would be well spoken of, learn to speak well of others. And, when you have learned to speak well of them, endeavour likewise to do well to them, and thus you will reap the fruit of being well spoken of by them.

Stoic   EPICTETUS

68

TALKING AND DOING

Will ye tell others to be righteous and not practise righteousness yourself?

Muslim   *Koran 2. 44*

69

THE ETERNAL LAW

Hatred is never diminished by hatred. Hatred is diminished by love. This is the eternal law.

Buddhist   *Dhammapada*

70

PILGRIM BROTHERS

Lord, help me faithfully to journey along my road, holding my rightful place in the great procession of humanity;

Help me above all to recognize you and to help you in all my pilgrim brothers.

Christian   MICHEL QUOIST

71

DIFFERING OPINIONS

When you meet those whose opinions differ from your own, do not turn away your face from them. All are seeking truth, and there are many roads leading thereto. Truth has many aspects, but it remains always and for ever one.

Bahai   ABDU'L-BAHA

72

PRAYER OF THE EMPEROR T'ANG

O supreme and sovereign God, let me know Thy will and pleasure. If I do sin against Thee let not my friends suffer for my sin. But if my friends sin against Thee let me bear the penalty of their iniquities.

Confucian

73

OUR DUTIES

Our duties are kindness towards all creatures, patience, humility, truth, purity, contentment, decorum of manners, gentleness of speech, friendliness, freedom from envy or avarice and the habit of speaking evil of others.

Hindu   *Vishnu Purana*

74

FOR ALL IN NEED

We beseech thee to hear us, O God, for all who are worn by illness; all who are wronged and oppressed; all who are suffering for righteousness' sake; the weary and heavy-laden; the aged and the dying, that they may be strengthened by thy might, consoled by thy love, and cherished by thy fatherly pity.

Christian   JOHN HUNTER

75

THE PAIN OF OTHERS

May my heart lend its ear to every cry of pain, like as the lotus bares its heart to drink the morning sun. Let not the fierce sun dry one tear of pain before I have wiped it from the sufferer's eye. But let each burning human tear drop on my heart and there remain, nor ever be brushed off until the pain that caused it is removed.

Buddhist   GOTAMA

76

THE GOOD MAN

He who calls those his own
Who are vexed and troubled,
God must surely dwell in him,
He that takes to his heart
One who has no protector
And shows to his servants
The same kindness which he shows to his sons —
He is the image of God.

Hindu   TUKARAMA

77

THREE RULES FOR A FRIEND

There are three rules which a friend should observe towards a friend, namely: Admonish him when at fault, cherish with a deep joy whatever good there is in him, stand by him in time of trouble . . . A friend should not be forsaken simply on the strength of some other person's evil report. If you hear your friend evilly spoken of, be all the more careful to find out the truth of the matter.

Buddhist   from scriptures

78

ENEMIES INTO FRIENDS

In the company of saints, man learns how to turn enemies into
    friends,
As he becomes completely free from evil,
And bears malice to none.
In the company of the good, there is no swerving from the path,
No looking down upon anybody as evil.
Man sees all round him the Lord of Supreme Joy,
And freeing himself from the feverish sense of self,
Abandons all pride.
Such is the efficacy of fellowship with a holy man, whose
    greatness is known only to the Lord:
The servant of the Ideal is akin to his Master.

Sikh   *Sukhmanu 7.3*

79

BE GENEROUS

Be generous in prosperity, and thankful in adversity. Be worthy of the trust of thy neighbour, and look upon him with a bright and friendly face. Be a treasure to the poor, an admonisher to the rich, an answerer of the cry of the needy, a preserver of the sanctity of thy pledge. Be fair in thy judgment, and guarded in thy speech. Be unjust to no man, and show all meekness to all men. Be as a lamp unto them that walk in darkness, a joy to the sorrowful, a sea for the thirsty, a haven for the distressed, an upholder and defender of the victim of oppression. Let integrity and uprightness distinguish all thine acts.

Bahai   BAHA'U'LLAH

80

RULES FOR RIGHT LIVING

Be pious towards God in private and in public; eat little, sleep little; speak little; depart from wickedness and sin; endure patiently the contumely of men; shun the company of the base and consort with the noble hearted. The best man is he that doeth good to men; and the best speech is that which is short and guideth men aright. Praise be to God who is the Unity.

Muslim   SHAMSU'D-DIN

81

MAKE YOUR HEART LOWLY

Sing the song with earnestness, making pure the heart;
If you would attain God, then this is an easy way.
Make your heart lowly, touch the feet of saints,
Of others do not hear the good or bad qualities, nor think
    of them.
. . . Be it much or little, do good to others.

Hindu   TUKARAMA

82

OUR FRIENDS

Be pleased, O Lord, to remember our friends, and all that have prayed for us, and that have done us good. Do thou good to them, and return all their kindness double, rewarding them with blessings, sanctifying them with thy graces, and at the last bringing them to glory.

Christian   JEREMY TAYLOR

83

THE LAW OF PIETY

May we truly follow the excellent Law of Piety—in many good deeds, compassion, liberality, truthfulness and purity.

Buddhist   ASOKA

84

O YE RICH

O ye rich ones on earth! The poor in your midst, are My trust; guard ye My trust, and be not intent only on your own ease.

Bahai   BAHA'U'LLAH

85

LOVER OF MANKIND

No one who is a Lover of Money, a Lover of Pleasure, or a Lover of Glory, is likewise a Lover of Mankind; but only he who is a Lover of Virtues.

Stoic   EPICTETUS

86

FOR THE DEAF

O God, give us sympathy for those who are deaf. They live in a silent world so remote and so different from ours. We take for granted speech and music and the ceaseless sounds of ordinary life—to them all is silence, they cannot even hear the voices of their dearest friends. We enjoy the song of birds, the splash of water, the rush of wind, the whispering of trees—to them all is silence. Give us sympathy, O God, and an eagerness to take into their silent world imaginative understanding and love, as you would have us do.

Christian   S.G.H.

87
YOURSELF, THEN OTHERS

Four things should always be kept in mind, namely: examine first yourself and then others; examine first your own troubles and then the troubles of others; examine first your own will and then the wills of others; examine first your own principles and then the principles of others.

Buddhist   *Advice to a Layman*

88
THE WORK OF HEALING

O Lord, the healer of all our diseases, who knowest how the sick have need of a physician, bless all whom thou hast called to be sharers in thine own work of healing with health alike of body and soul; that they may learn their art in dependence upon thee, and exercise it always under thy sanction, and to thy honour and glory.

Christian   *Sursum Corda*

89
DUST AGAINST THE WIND

For an evil man to slander a wise man is like spitting at the heavens; the spit will never reach the heavens but only fall on the face of the spitter. And again it is like throwing dust against the wind which ends in being blown against the one who tries it. He who reviles the wise only brings calamity upon himself.

Buddhist   from Chinese scriptures

90
FOR THE PARALYSED AND HANDICAPPED

Make us, O God, to appreciate our own privileges. We have full use of our limbs and strength to move and do as we will, and so we ask thy blessings on those who are denied these things. May our sympathy always go out to the paralysed and the handicapped who cannot share the varied and strenuous joys which make our lives so full and happy. Show us how to give friendship and help to deprived ones, in the true spirit of Jesus our Lord.

Christian   S.G.H.

91

MEN AND WOMEN

The believers, men and women, are protecting friends
one of another.

Muslim   *Koran 9. 72*

92

LOOKING FOR THE GOOD

Remembering that everywhere and in all people can be found some sort of faith and righteousness, may we seek to foster this, and not destroy. May we not look for evil in one another, but for good.

Buddhist   ASOKA

93

GRANT US GOOD FELLOWSHIP

Grant, Lord, to those assembled here, such purity of heart and clearness of sight, that they may seek and find all that is best in others. Grant us charity, that we may feel with others in their failures. Grant us good fellowship, that we may help others to put right whatever is done amiss; and for ourselves grant both the desire and the strength to live up to the best that is in us.

Christian   *Hymns and Prayers for Dragons*

94

LEARN TO DO GOOD

Cleansing my own heart, looking not to the failures or misdeeds of others, but rather to my own omissions and misdeeds, may I cease to do evil and learn to do good.

Buddhist   from scriptures

95

BORN FOR CO-OPERATION

Say to thyself, at dawn: today I shall run up against the busy-body, the ungrateful, the overbearing, the deceitful, the envious, the self-centred. All this has fallen to their lot because they are ignorant of good and evil. But I, understanding the nature of the Good, that it is fair, and of Evil, that it is ugly, and the nature of the evil-doer himself, that he is my kin—as sharing, not indeed the same blood and seed, but intelligence and a spark of the Divine—can neither be damaged by any of them (for no one can involve me in what is disgraceful) nor can be angry with my kinsman or estranged from him. For we have been born for co-operation, as have feet, hands, eyelids and the rows of upper and lower teeth. Therefore to thwart one another is unnatural; and we do thwart one another when we shew resentment and dislike.

Stoic   MARCUS AURELIUS

96

ACCIDENT AND ILLNESS

O God, we remember before Thee the needs of those who are victims of accident and illness; we remember all hospitals and houses of healing, all chaplains, doctors, and nurses. Bless their labours in the service of their fellows, to the good of those they serve, and the greater glory of Thy holy name.

Christian   A.W. SAWYER

97

FOR ALL IN PAIN

Dear Lord, for all in pain
We pray to Thee;
O come and smite again
Thine enemy.

Give to thy servants skill
To soothe and bless,
And to the tired and ill
Give quietness.

And, Lord, to those who know
Pain may not cease,
Come near, that even so
They may have peace.

Christian   AMY WILSON CARMICHAEL

98

LOVE

Show love to all creatures and thou wilt be happy, for when thou lovest all things thou lovest the Lord, for he is all in all.

Hindu   TULSI DAS

99

FUTURE LIFE

First in the Blessed Pure Land
When I attain my birth,
Shall be the precious memory
Of friends I left on earth.

Buddhist   HONEN SHONIN

100

CHILD SUFFERERS

O God, our Father, we remember before Thee all orphaned, homeless, and unwanted children, the children of loveless homes, and those who suffer from bodily defect and disease. Make our hearts burn within us for the children of our dark places, and teach us how to turn to good account the laws that protect them and the efforts of those who strive to succour them.

Christian   Mothers' Union

YOURSELF

. . . and lead us not into temptation,
but deliver us from evil . . .

101

LIKE A LITTLE FISH

Lord, Thou mighty River, all-knowing, all-seeing,
And I like a little fish in Thy great waters,
How shall I sound Thy depths?
How shall I reach Thy shores?
Wherever I go, I see Thee only,
And snatched out of Thy waters, I die of separation.
I know not the fisher, I see not the net,
But flapping in my agony, I call upon Thee for help.
O Lord who pervades all things,
In my folly I thought Thee far,
But no deed I do can ever be out of Thy sight.

Sikh   GURU NANAK

102

IF I AM RIGHT

If I am right, Thy grace impart,
    Still in the right to stay;
If I am wrong, O teach my heart
    To find that better way!

Christian   ALEXANDER POPE

103

IF GOD WILLS

God hath commanded:
Couple the word 'If God wills' with all your vows,
Because the governance of all is in my hands.
Each day I am engaged in a fresh work,
There is naught that swerves from my purpose.

Sufi   JELALEDDIN RUMI

104

THE HOUSE OF MY SOUL

O Lord, the house of my soul is narrow; enlarge it that thou mayest enter in. It is ruinous, O repair it! It displeases thy sight; I confess it, I know. But who shall cleanse it, or to whom shall I cry but unto thee? Cleanse me from my secret faults, O Lord, and spare thy servant from strange sins.

Christian   ST. AUGUSTINE

105

THE FLAME WHICH GLOWS

O Lord, to find Thee is my desire
But to comprehend Thee
Is beyond my strength.
Remembering Thee is solace
To my sorrowing heart,
Thoughts of Thee are my Constant Companions
I call upon Thee night and day.
The flame of Thy love glows
In the darkness of my night.

Sufi   ABDULLAH ANSARI

106

THE DIVINE COURT OF HOLINESS

Purge thy heart from malice, and, innocent of envy, enter the divine court of holiness.

Bahai   BAHA'U'LLAH

107

INDIFFERENCE TO WORLDLY CIRCUMSTANCES

At one time one may carry water.
At another time one may repose upon a couch:
As occasion comes so must one be.
At one time many dishes
At another time dry bread.

At one time riding in a carriage
At another time on bare feet.
At one time splendid robes,
At another time worn-out garments.
At one time all riches,
At another time the endurance of poverty.
At one time the companionship of the good,
At another time connection with the bad.
. . . Know that happiness and misery are indifferent.

Hindu   TUKARAMA

108

GIVING AND GETTING

The more we give the more we have.

Taoist   LAO TSE

109

THE NAME

Cultivate thy mind with the Name
And it will leave off wandering and be at rest,
No harm can touch a man who feels the indwelling presence of God.
The age is burning hot: the Name alone can create a cooling
    atmosphere;
Cherish it, O cherish it, that you may attain a lasting peace.
Love and devotion enlighten the mind,
Fear departs and hope comes to fill the outlook,
The fetters of death are shaken off,
And man reaches the estate of immortality.

Sikh   *Sukhmanu* 19.3

110

FOR TRANQUILLITY

Dispose my soul for tranquillity, O God, that the loving knowledge of
contemplation may the more grow and my soul will feel it and relish it
more than all other things whatever; because it brings with it peace and
rest, sweetness and delight, without trouble.

Christian   ST. JOHN OF THE CROSS

111

HOW SIN COMES

All sin comes from the mouth that speaks untruth and from the heart that denies the future world.

Buddhist   from scriptures

112

SINS OF OUR IGNORANCE

Forgive, O Lord, these three sins of my ignorance:
    Thou art everywhere, but I worship you here;
    Thou art without form; but I worship you in forms that I see;
    Thou needest no praise; yet I offer you now prayers and
    salutations.

Hindu

113

MEDITATION

The sign from God in contemplation is silence, because it is impossible for a man to do two things at one time—he cannot both speak and meditate.

Through the faculty of meditation man attains to eternal life; through it he receives the breath of the Holy Spirit—the bestowal of the Spirit is given in reflection and meditation.

Meditation is the key for opening the doors of mysteries. In that state man abstracts himself; in that state man withdraws himself from all outside objects; in that subjective mood he is immersed in the ocean of spiritual life and can unfold the secrets of things-in-themselves. To illustrate this, think of man as endowed with two kinds of sight; when the power of insight is being used the outward power of vision does not see.

The faculty of meditation frees man from the animal nature, discerns the reality of things, puts man in touch with God.

Through this faculty man enters into the very Kingdom of God.

Bahai   ABDU'L-BAHA

114

TO THE UTMOST OF THY POWER

If in every particular action thou dost perform what is fitting to the utmost of thy power, let it suffice thee. And who can hinder thee, but that thou mayest perform what is fitting? But there may be some outward let and impediment. Not any, that can hinder thee, but that whatsoever thou dost thou may do it justly, temperately, and with the praise of God.

Stoic   MARCUS AURELIUS

115

SO GO THOU FORTH

As a beggar goes a-begging,
Bowl in one hand, staff in the other,
Rings in his ears, in ashes smothered,
So go thou forth in life.
With earrings made of contentment,
With modesty thy begging bowl,
Meditation the fabric of thy garment,
Knowledge of death thy cowl.
Let thy mind be chaste, virginal clean,
Faith the staff on which to lean.
Thou shalt then thy fancy humiliate
With mind subdued the world subjugate.

Sikh   *Japji 28*

116

LIKE A HUGE MAD ELEPHANT

The heart is fickle and capricious, and it is hard to control and pacify. It rushes like a huge mad elephant; its thoughts fly quickly like flashes of lightning; it is restless and noisy like a monkey. Thus it is the root of all evil.

Buddhist   from scriptures

117

HOW ERROR COMES

When the Creator gives men the faculty of judgment they abandon error and become enamoured of the truth; but, conquered by time, temperament, or fate, even the good, as a result of their humanity, may err from virtue.

Hindu   TULSI DAS

118

I WAS FOUND OF THEE

I said, 'I will find God,' and forth I went
To seek Him in the clearness of the sky,
But over me stood unendurably
Only a pitiless, sapphire firmament
Ringing the world — blank splendour; yet intent
Still to find God, 'I will go seek,' said I,
'His way upon the waters,' and drew nigh
An ocean marge weed-strewn, and foam besprent;
And the waves dashed on idle sand and stone,
And very vacant was the long, blue sea;
But in the evening as I sat alone,
My window open to the vanishing day,
Dear God! I could not choose but kneel and pray,
And it sufficed that I was found of Thee.

Christian   EDWARD DOWDEN

119

IN THY HEART

God is in thy heart, yet thou searchest for him in the wilderness.

Sikh   *The Granth*

120

A HEAVENLY CIVILIZATION

Use your knowledge always for the benefit of others.

Let your ambition be the achievement on earth of a Heavenly Civilization.

Bahai   ABDU'L-BAHA

121

FRIENDSHIPS

Friendship with the upright, friendship with the sincere,
and friendship with the man of much observation:
These three friendships are advantageous.

Confucian

122

A PLEDGE

I with thy help O God!
Denounce disobedience and the evil mind.

Zoroastrian

123

A CLEAN TONGUE

Help me to remember, Lord, that he who has a clean heart has also a clean tongue.

Christian

124

WE MAKE OURSELVES

We are what we have made and our future is made by us now.

Jain   MAHAVIRA

125

IN HARMONY WITH HEAVEN

May we be in 'harmony with heaven and earth; in brightness, with the sun and moon; in orderly procedure, with the four seasons; and in relation of what is fortunate and what is calamitous, with the operations of Providence.'

Confucian adapted

126

AT LIFE'S END

The world, O my brother, abideth with no one;
Fix thy heart on Him who created it, that is enough,
Place not reliance or trust in Fortune . . .
When the pure soul is on the point of departing, what mattereth
  it whether it be on a throne or on the bare ground?

Muslim SADI

127

SIMPLY FOLLOWING THEE

O Lord and Master of us all, whate'er our name or sign, we own thy sway, we hear thy call, we test our lives by thine.

Our thoughts lie open to thy sight, and naked to thy glance; our secret sins are in the light of thy pure countenance.

Our friend, our brother, and our Lord, what may thy service be? Nor name, nor sign, nor ritual word, but simply following thee!

Christian JOHN GREENLEAF WHITTIER

128

CALM

Put away all anxiety and fix your thoughts on the good God.

Hindu TULSI DAS

129

EVIL WITHIN ME

O Lord! I am afraid of the evil within me.
Teach me how to save myself
From the snares of self;
Take me by the hand,
For without thy mercy I have no refuge.

Sufi   ABDULLAH ANSARI

130

GOD BE IN MY HEAD

God be in my head, and in my understanding;
God be in my eyes, and in my looking;
God be in my mouth, and in my speaking;
God be in my heart, and in my thinking;
God be at my end, and at my departing.

Christian   *Sarum Primer*

131

FIGHTING FOR TRUTH

O Lord, grant me this boon,
That I may never shirk a chance to do the right.
I may never fear my enemy when I come out to fight for the truth
And I may always believe that I will win.
I may be guided by my conscience
And I may ever be hungry for chanting Thy praises.
O Lord grant me the boon that when my end draws near,
I may fall fighting for truth.

Sikh   GURU GOBIND SINGH

132

VOICE OF THE HUMBLE

Thou . . . Lord of him that is silent;
Who comes at the voice of the humble man,
I call upon Thee when I am in distress,
And Thou comest that thou mayest save me;
That Thou mayest give breath to him that is wretched,
That Thou mayest save me who am in bondage.

Egyptian   1300 B.C.

133

NOT ALONE

When I have shut my door and darkened my room let me not say that I
am alone. You, God, are with me, and need no light to see what I do.

Stoic   EPICTETUS (adapted)

134

SERVICE

This is my prayer to thee, my Lord—give me the strength to make my
love fruitful in service.

Hindu   TAGORE

135

LORD WE BELIEVE

Lord we believe, but would believe more firmly. We hope, but would
hope more securely. We love, but would love more warmly. By thy
wisdom do thou direct us, by thy righteousness do thou keep us, by thy
sweet mercy comfort and protect us.

Let pride never corrupt us, nor flattery move us, nor evil entice us
from thee.

Grant us grace to cleanse our memories, to check our tongues, to restrain our senses.

Let us overcome love of pleasure by self-denial, love of money by freely giving, heat of temper by gentleness.

Make us prudent in counsel, steadfast in danger, patient in adversity, humble in prosperity, temperate in meat and drink, diligent in duty, careful for others.

Let us learn from thee, O God, how little is all that is earthly, how great all that is heavenly; how short all that is of time, how lasting all that is of eternity.

Christian   *Treasury of Devotions*

136

ONE TONGUE, TWO EARS

Nature has given Man one tongue but two ears, that we may hear twice as much as we speak.

If you always remember that God stands by, an inspector of whatever you do, either in Body or Soul; you will never err, either in your prayers or actions; and you will have God abiding with you.

Stoic   EPICTETUS

137

RIGHT MOTIVES

O my Lord, if I worship thee from fear of Hell, burn me in hell; if I worship thee from hope of Paradise, shut me out from Paradise. But if I worship thee for thine own sake, then withhold not from me thine eternal Beauty.

Sufi   RABIAH

138

CLEAN HEART AND RIGHT SPIRIT

Have mercy upon me, O God, according to thy loving kindness; according unto the multitude of thy tender mercies blot out my transgressions. Wash me thoroughly from mine iniquity, and cleanse me from my sin. For I acknowledge my transgressions; and my sin is ever before me. Create in me a clean heart, O God; and renew a right spirit within me. O Lord, open Thou my lips; and my mouth shall show forth thy praise.

Jewish   *Psalm 51*

139

THE STRINGS OF MY LUTE

O my merciful Father, upon life's long and tiring road, ever I am weary and confused, please lend me your loving hand and endearing touch.

In my deluded egotism, if ever for a moment I fall away from your holy laws, O my Lord of Lords, forsake me not, that I may return to you again. I am a deluded creature, your foolish child, forgive my faults and keep me ever at your (lotus) feet.

If the sweet voice of enticements sings to me and leads me down the slippery path of error and I forget your sacred memory, O my Lord of Life, receive me once more to your loving breast.

If the harshness of the world makes life unbearable, O Beloved, touch me with your refreshing hand, subdue the consuming flame of my life and give my spirit thy holy peace.

What should I say, how must I pray, my Star of Life whose light dwells within me? You know every ripple of my thoughts; they are better known to you than to me.

With sobbing heart and tearful eyes I make this submission at your holy feet. O Father, that in waking or sleeping, in life and in death, may my body and heart respond to thy divine will.

Let the strings of my lute quiver with your music and all my heart be radiant with your glory.

Hindu   MIRA

140

REALITY OF GOD

How long wilt thou give the reins into the hand of Doubt?
For every one there is a pathway and approach to God;
To every one is pledged the certainty of His existence;
On the heart of every thoughtful man is painted His image,

And for every painting there must be a painter ...
When thou beholdest before thee the architecture of the universe
How is it that thy mind is not busied with the Architect?
When thou seest the work, turn thy face towards the Workman.

Muslim   JAMI

141

MATTER IN ONE MIND

I have seen God within me,
And His Name tastes sweet to me.
The whole world of Matter is contained within one Mind,
Although it appears so various in colour and form.
The ambrosial Name of God is the source of all conceivable joys;
It lives in the body;
And the strains of its divine music are heard in the silent
        recesses of the heart.
The ecstasy of its wonder cannot be described:
It can only be felt by those who are granted the vision.
They alone can conceive it.

Sikh   *Sukhmanu 23.*1

142

SELF CONQUEST

Though one should conquer in battle a thousand times a thousand men,
he who conquers himself is the greatest warrior.

Buddhist   from scriptures

143

BE THOU NE'ER AFRAID

... So ill was ne'er by God designed
To bloom on earth, and govern human kind:
Ah, no, real evils live not, here below—
Man makes his ills, man bids his sorrows flow.

From righteous acts let nought thy mind dissuade:
Of vulgar censures be thou ne'er afraid
Pursue the task which justice doth decree,
E'en tho' the crowd think different from thee!

Stoic   EPICTETUS

144

HELP THOU OUR UNBELIEF

Lord, we believe in thee, help thou our unbelief; we love thee, yet not
with perfect hearts as we would; we long for thee, yet not with our full
strength; we trust in thee, yet not with our whole mind. Accept our
faith, our love, our longing to know and serve thee, our trust in thy
power to keep us. What is cold do thou kindle, what is lacking do thou
supply.

Christian   MALCOLM SPENCER

145

LOVE FILLS THE UNIVERSE

Give me, O God, ears to hear that the flute of the universe is played
without ceasing, and its sound is love.

Sikh   KABIR

146

THE SAINTS OF EVERY FAITH

Love the saints of every faith;
Put away thy pride;
Remember, the essence of religion
Is meekness and sympathy,
Not fine clothes,
Not the Yogi's garb and ashes,
Not the blowing of the horn,
Not the shaven head,
Not long prayers,
Not recitations and torturings,
Not the ascetic way,
But a life of goodness and purity,
Amid the world's temptations.

Sikh   GURU NANAK

147

HONEST AIMS

To honest aims let all thy actions tend—
Truth, justice, peace, their purpose and their end.

Greek   PYTHAGORAS

148

CONTROL OF SELF

Teach us, O Blessed One, control of speech, control of thought, control of action. Help us to keep these roads of action clear and so find the Way made known by Thee to the wise in heart.

Buddhist   from scriptures

149

SINS OF MY YOUTH

Forgive me my sins, O Lord, forgive me the sins of my youth and mine age, the sins of my soul and the sins of my body, my secret and my whispering sins, my presumptuous and my crying sins, the sins that I have done to please myself, and the sins that I have done to please others. Forgive me those sins which I know and those which I know not; forgive them, O Lord, forgive them all, of thy great goodness.

Christian   BISHOP WILSON

150

ALL ARE LIKE YOU

Every man and woman that has ever been born is of the same nature as yourself. He, whose is the world, and whose are all its children, He is my Guru, my Lord.

Sikh   KABIR

151

HEAR AND SEE NO EVIL

Hear no evil, and see no evil, abase not thyself, neither sigh and weep. Speak no evil, that thou mayest not hear it spoken unto thee, and magnify not the faults of others that thine own faults may not appear great; and wish not the abasement of anyone, that thine own abasement be not exposed. Live then the days of thy life, that are less than a fleeting moment, with thy mind stainless, thy heart unsullied, thy thoughts pure, and thy nature sanctified, so that, free and content, thou mayest put away this mortal frame and repair unto the mystic paradise, and abide in the eternal kingdom for evermore.

Bahai   BAHA'U'LLAH

152

HOW BEST TO SERVE GOD

Strive after those enjoyments which are eternal.
For earthly enjoyments will pass away . . .
Incline thine affections to learning and knowledge
For these must show thee thy way toward God.
Do not let thy words go beyond measure,
For thou art but a young creature, and the world is old.

Muslim   FERDUSI

153

THE SUNLIGHT OF TRUTH

May we learn to think without prejudice, love all beings for love's sake, express our convictions fearlessly, lead a life of purity, so that the sunlight of truth will illuminate us. If theology and dogma stand in our way in the search for truth let them be put aside. May we be earnest and work out our salvation with diligence so that the fruits of holiness will be ours.

Buddhist   ANAGARIKA DHARMAPALA, at the World's
Parliament of Religions, Chicago, 1893

154

CONQUERING ONESELF

O God, help me to victory over myself, for difficult to conquer is oneself, though when that is conquered all is conquered.

Jain   from scriptures

155

THOU SHINEST IN EVERYTHING

It is Thy sweet joy, O Lord, that fills my heart; it is Thy silent peace that reigns over my mind. All is repose, force, concentration, light and serenity; is it only the earth or the whole world that lives in me, I know not, but it is Thou, O Lord, who dwellest in this consciousness and givest life to it; it is Thou who seest, Thou who knowest, Thou who doest. It is Thou alone whom I see everywhere, or rather there is no longer any 'I', all is one and this Oneness, it is Thou.

Glory to Thee, O Lord, Master of the world. Thou shinest in everything!

Hindu   SRI AUROBINDO

156

WHEN I SURVEY THE WONDROUS CROSS

When I survey the wondrous Cross
   On which the Prince of Glory died,
My richest gain I count but loss,
   And pour contempt on all my pride.

See, from His head, His hands, His feet,
   Sorrow and love flow mingled down;
Did e'er such love and sorrow meet,
   Or thorns compose so rich a crown?

Were the whole realm of nature mine,
   That were an offering far too small;
Love so amazing, so divine,
   Demands my soul, my life, my all.

Christian   ISAAC WATTS

157

HOW PUNY A PART

Think of the totality of all Being, and what a mite of it is yours; think of all Time, and the brief fleeting instant of it that is allotted to yourself; think of Destiny, and how puny a part of it you are.

Stoic   MARCUS AURELIUS

158

PRECEPTS INTO PRACTICE

Show us, O Blessed One, that though we can recite but little of the Teaching, yet put its Precepts into practice, ridding ourselves of craving and delusion, and possessed of knowledge and serenity of mind, cleaving to nothing in this or any other world, then we are true disciples of Thee, O Blessed One.

Buddhist   thoughts on The Way

159

BE STILL

Expend not a breath in idle conversation,
Put a seal on thy talk—*God is the Greatest!*

Muslim   JAMI

160

OUR WORK AND AMBITIONS

We pray, Father, God, for our work, our ambitions, our plans for the future. Whatever our hand findeth to do may we do it with our might. Let our ambitions be not selfish, in order that we may grasp much for ourselves, but rather be an eagerness to use to the full whatever talents you have given us, so that muscles and limbs and minds and souls may be stretched to the utmost, and we can truly give of our best to this world and to our fellows—because so much has been given to us.

Christian   S.G.H.

161

UNIVERSAL AND TRUE

Bring us into living union with Thee. Give us aspiration for what is universal and true, drawing us to light, to love, to joy and beauty, and to refined purity of being.

Hindu   SRI AUROBINDO

162

TRUE PHILOSOPHY

The effect of true philosophy, God be thanked, is unaffected simplicity and modesty, so may I not be persuaded to ostentation and vain glory.

Stoic   MARCUS AURELIUS

163

REFLECTION AND THOUGHTLESSNESS

Reflection is the path of immortality, thoughtlessness the path of death. Those who are vigilant do not die; those who are thoughtless are as already dead.

Buddhist   *Dhammapada*

164

YOUR SORROWS WILL VANISH

O my Soul, forever abide with God.
Abide with God, O my Soul, and all your sorrows will vanish.
You will be acceptable to God and He will conduct all your affairs.
The Perfect Lord is omnipotent, why should you forget Him?
O my Soul, forever abide with God.

Sikh   GURU AMAR DAS

165

MINE EYES ACHE

O Lord, who art the Giver of joy and the Dispeller of
sorrow, mine eyes ache when there is no sight of Thee.

Hindu   MIRA

166

NOT TO BE ANXIOUS

O Lord Jesus Christ, who has told us not to be anxious, we trust ourselves and our loved ones to thy loving care, knowing that round about and underneath are the everlasting arms, and praying Thee to give us now and always that peace which the world cannot give, nor take away, but which comes only from the Father and from Thee, our Saviour and Friend.

Christian   *A Book of Prayers*

167

PANSIL

Praise to the Lord, the perfectly enlightened Buddha, the
    All-Enlightened One.
Praise to the Lord, the perfectly enlightened Buddha, the
    All-Enlightened One.
Praise to the Lord, the perfectly enlightened Buddha, the
    All-Enlightened One.
        I go to the Buddha for Refuge,
        I go to the Doctrine for Refuge,
        I go to the Order for Refuge.
        Again I go to the Buddha for Refuge,
        Again I go to the Doctrine for Refuge,
        Again I go to the Order for Refuge.
        A third time I go to the Buddha for Refuge
        A third time I go to the Doctrine for Refuge,
        A third time I go to the Order for Refuge.
    I undertake the rule of training to refrain from killing
or harming living things.
    I undertake the rule of training to refrain from taking
that which is not given.
    I undertake the rule of training to refrain from licentiousness
in sensual pleasures.
    I undertake the rule of training to refrain from falsehood.
    I undertake the rule of training to refrain from liquors
which engender slothfulness.

Buddhist   'Pansil', recited in Buddhist
                                           devotions, with the 'Refuge
                                          Formula'

168

FILLED WITH GOODNESS

Pray to God and fill your heart with his pleasure so that you may be sure to be filled with goodness by Him.

Zoroastrian   *Zend-Avesta*

169

WHAT HAPPENED YESTERDAY

O Lord I am afraid of myself,
From Thee flows good alone,
From me flows evil.

Each day I recall the day
That is left behind.
Sorrowing over my misdeeds
The thought of thy mercy
Is the only solace of my heart.

Others fear what the morrow may bring;
I am afraid of what happened yesterday.

Sufi   ABDULLAH ANSARI

170

HOLD NOT OUR SINS UP

Father in Heaven! Hold not our sins up against us but hold us up against our sins, so that the thought of Thee when it wakens in our soul, and each time it wakens, should not remind us of what we have committed but of what Thou didst forgive, not of how we went astray but of how Thou didst save us.

Christian   SOREN KIERKEGAARD

171

A BEGINNING

Wouldst thou be good, then first believe that thou art evil.

Before all other things it is needful to learn that God is, and taketh thought for all things; and that nothing can be had from him, neither deeds, nor even thoughts or wishes...If the Divine is faithful, so must he who would please Him be faithful too; if free, so must he be free; if beneficent, so must he be beneficent; if high-minded, so must he be high-minded; so that thus follow therefrom.

Stoic   EPICTETUS

172

LONELY ROAD OF LEARNING

Take me aside, O God, and let me be
A little while within Thy company.

And speak to me, although no word is spoken
And still the silence closes round, unbroken.

And lead me for my spiritual discerning
Further along thy lonely road of learning.

And let me hold communion, Thou and I,
With minds outreaching, and the world put by.

Christian   HILDA M. ORCHARD

173

LIKE THE LOTUS STEM

How can the bond between Thee and me be severed?
Like the lotus stem that dwells in water do I dwell in Thee.

Hindu   MIRA

174

DAY AND NIGHT

I will celebrate Thy praise, Lord of heaven and earth, when I rise up, and praise Thee in the night season, and when the stars begin to disappear.

Muslim   *Koran* (adapted)

175

I OUGHT, BUT I HAVE NOT

God All-Seeing:
I ought to have thought, but I have not thought;
I ought to have spoken, but I have not spoken;
I ought to have acted, but I have not acted—as it
was the will of thy Good Spirit. I repent for that sin
with thought, word and deed.

I ought not to have thought, but I have thought;
I ought not to have spoken, but I have spoken;
I ought not to have acted, but I have acted, as it
was the will of the Evil Spirit. I repent of that sin
with my thought, word and deed.

Zoroastrian

GRATITUDE

. . . Our Father . . .

176

FATHER, WE THANK THEE

Father,
We thank Thee that dark and uncertain is our future,
Because, in darkness and doubt,
We must cling more closely to Thee.

Father,
We thank Thee that there will be pain,
Because through pain we are forced to clutch at Thy hand.

Father,
We thank Thee that there will be loneliness,
Because in loneliness Thou art more surely our Friend.

Father,
We thank Thee that there shall be death,
Because dying we come unto Thee.

Christian   JOHN S. HOYLAND

177

GIVE ME, O LORD

O Lord, give me a heart
That I may pour it out in thanksgiving.
Give me life
That I may spend it
In working for the salvation of the world.

O Lord, give me that right discrimination
That the lure of the world may cheat me no more.
Give me the strength
That my faith suffer no eclipse.

O Lord, give me understanding,
That I stray not from the path.
Give me light
To avoid pitfalls.

Sufi   ABDULLAH ANSARI

178

PROCLAIM HIM

Our Lord has come, let us pray that he may forgive us our sins.

He gave light with his light to our lamps. Put oil into them by your faith. Proclaim him.

He gave the bread of life to the hungry, the clothing he brought to the naked. Proclaim him.

He gave light by his love to our intelligence; he made his faith shine in our reason. Proclaim him.

He sounded with his trumpet in the worlds that are far, that are near, he roused them. Proclaim him.

They shut him up in their prisons and loaded his limbs with iron. We proclaim him.

Let us bless him now, my brethren, and sing to him in our spirit. Proclaim him.

Do not make reckoning with us now, our Lord, according to the multitude of our sins.

Glory to the Father. Proclaim him.

Manichaean   *Psalm 228*

179

GOD'S CARE FOR US

There is no need to place the child in the mother's hands—
By her own instinct she draws it to her;
Why should I take thought? He whose business it is will be responsible.
Without its asking the mother keeps sweet things for the child,
When it is engaged in play she seeks and brings it;
Sitting down, she presses it close to her breast,
When it is sick she is restless as the parched corn in the fire.
. . . Take no thought for your own body—
The mother will not allow the child to be hurt.

Hindu   TUKARAMA

180

THOSE WHO PERISH SOON

Those who pray for worldly objects
Shall perish soon.
But those who worship the Supreme Being,
When they meet the Guru, shall live forever.
With love and devotion in their hearts,
They are awake every day and night singing God's praises.
Those who are destined to receive God's gifts, He takes by
    the arm and blends with Himself.

Sikh   GURU ARJAN

181

MIRACULOUS GIFT

I pray for a gift which perhaps would be miraculous: simply to be able
to see that field of waving grass as I should see it if association and the
'film of custom' did not obscure it.

Christian   MARK RUTHERFORD

182

BEING CONTENT

He who does not know how to be content with what he has is poor,
however rich he may be; but he who has learned to be content is rich
even though he may have very little...Excessive wants are the seat of
suffering; and the labour of weariness of this world of life and death
arise from covetousness. He who wants little and so is above the
concerns of this life is perfectly free both as to body and
mind...Contentment is the domain of wealth and pleasure, of peace and
rest. The contented man is happy even though his bed is the bare
ground; while the man who knows not the secret of being content is
not satisfied even when dwelling in heavenly places.

Buddhist   from scriptures

183

THE GREAT ABODE

My mind is fixed on the Great Abode; it flies from the desires
of the world.
It is not of a shallow pool that I have any thought—who
goes to a little puddle for water?
Nor do I have any concern with the Ganga and the Jamuna.
Straight I go to the ocean.
With the intermediaries I have no business. I shall petition
the King directly.
I deal not in glass or lead or in iron which only makes a
heavy load.
Nor do I deal in silver or gold—I am dealer only in
diamonds.
O it is my great fortune that the Ocean has befriended me.
The Lord Himself has granted His acquaintance, and unfolded
His treasure to me.

Hindu   MIRA

184

ADVERSITY IS A MEDICINE

Adversity is a medicine and comfort a disease,
because in comfort there is no yearning for God.

Sikh   *Asa di Var 12.*1

185

THE FIRST THING TO LEARN

The first thing to learn is that there is a God. Then, O God, that Thy
knowledge pervades the whole universe, extending not only to our acts
but to our thoughts and feelings. To have Thee for our Maker and
Father and Guardian, should not this free us from all sadness and fear?

Stoic   EPICTETUS

186

TREES

For the strength and peace of the trees,
We thank Thee, our God:

For their quiet unhasting growth,
For their stalwart and trusty friendship,
For their sociable neighbourly silence:

For their ancient calm on a windless day:

For their cheery, murmurous stir
When the breeze is abroad with its melodies:

For the quiet and sure revelation of Thee
Which they bring to our souls
As we sit thus silent amongst them,
We thank Thee, Our God.

Christian   JOHN S. HOYLAND

187

THE GENTLE ARMS PROTECT ME

The pure touch of Thy love divine
Hath washed away all my sins,
Thy grace hath wiped away the past
From now a new life begins.

Thy holy presence I feel all around,
Thy gentle arms protect me;
I know now, Thou failest never—
Those who trustingly look to Thee.

Thy mercy is my stronghold,
My refuge, my strength, my stay;
Thy love is my life-giving nectar
That blesses and sustains me day to day.

O source of joy! O fount of bliss! My only prayer—
May I never stray from Thee,
The peace and comfort found in Thy love
May eternally remain with me.

Sikh   SURJIT J. SINGH

188

I PRAY WITH JOY

Omniscient Lord, lifting up my hands in all humility to Thee who art
Invisible and Munificent, I pray with joy for righteous actions, for
benevolent thoughts, so that I may thereby let the Soul of the Universe
rejoice.

Zoroastrian

189

WITH HEART OF FAITH

God has no voice, his form is unseen. With Him there is neither night
nor day, neither far nor near. Pray to Him simply, with a heart of faith.
He is your friend.

Shinto   BUNJIRO

190

O SACRED HEAD SORE WOUNDED

O sacred head sore wounded, with grief and pain bowed down, how
scornfully surrounded with thorns, Thy only crown! How pale art Thou
with anguish, with sore abuse and scorn! How does that visage languish
which once was bright as morn!

What language shall I borrow to thank Thee, dearest Friend, for this
Thy dying sorrow, Thy pity without end? Lord, make me Thine for
ever, nor let me faithless prove; O let me never, never abuse such dying
love!

Be near when I am dying; O show Thyself to me; and, for my
succour flying, come, Lord, to set me free: These eyes, new faith
receiving, from Jesus shall not move; for he who dies believing dies
safely through Thy love.

Christian   PAULUS GERHARDT

191

GOD ALONE

No one speaks by his own strength . . . the voice is His.
The cuckoo utters a sweet note.
But He that teaches her is Another.
How should I, poor wretch, make answer?
The Lord of the world has given me power of utterance.

Hindu   TUKARAMA

192

AIR AMPLER AND PURER

O God, to Thee we owe our life and the joys that weave themselves into it; to Thee we owe our loved ones, with all the delight of their companionship. Thy goodness has clothed the world in glorious raiment, and given us the power to feel its splendour. To Thee we owe the pleasures of the mind, the joy of books and the ennobling influence of art. And to Thee we owe, above all, the instinctive sense of Thy presence, the stir of the spirit which bids us seek after Thee, the aspirations which lift us above the lesser concerns of life into an air ampler and purer.

Jewish   *Liberal Prayer Book*

193

THE FOOTFALL OF AN ANT

Pray unto Him in any way you like. He is sure to hear you, for He can hear even the footfall of an ant.

Hindu   SRI RAMAKRISHNA

194

THIS UNIVERSE, OUR HOME

O God, we thank thee for this universe, our great home; for its vastness and its riches, and for the manifoldness of the life which teems upon it and of which we are part. We praise thee for the arching sky and the blessed winds, for the driving clouds and for the constellations on high. We praise thee for the salt sea and running water, for the everlasting

hills, for the trees and for the grass under our feet. We thank thee for
our senses by which we can see the splendour of the morning and hear
the jubilant songs of love, and smell the breath of the springtime. Grant
us, we pray thee, a heart wide open to all this joy and beauty, and save
our souls from being so steeped in care, or so darkened by passion, that
we pass heedless and unseeing when even the thornbush by the wayside
is aflame with the glory of God.

Christian   WALTER RAUSCHENBUSCH

195

IT IS THOU WHO UNITEST MEN

When man meeteth the Friend, he obtaineth happiness.
O God, Thou art the Friend; Thou art wise.
It is Thou who unitest men with Thee.

Sikh   GURU NANAK

196

MY GUIDE AND MY REFUGE

O God, refresh and gladden my spirit. Purify my heart. Illumine my
mind. I lay all my affairs in Thy hand. Thou art my Guide and my
Refuge. I will no longer be sorrowful and grieved, I will be happy and
joyful. O God, I will no longer be full of anxiety, nor will I let trouble
harass me. I will not dwell on the unpleasant things of life. O God!
Thou art kinder to me than I am to myself. I dedicate myself to Thee,
O Lord.

Bahai   ABDU'L-BAHA

197

WHERE OTHERS KNEEL

Bow down and worship where others kneel, for where so many have
been paying the tribute of adoration the kind Lord must manifest
Himself, for He is all mercy.

Hindu   SRI RAMAKRISHNA

198

HE WILL LEAD MANKIND

Let us praise the Lord of all, who is the Maker of heaven and earth. He was the guide of our fathers through all the ages; and He will lead mankind unto the time when the knowledge of Him and obedience to His laws shall fill the hearts of all men. He is our God, there is none else.

Jewish   *Service of the Heart*

199

CALL TO PRAYER

God's goodness hath been great to thee;
Let never day or night unhallowed pass,
But still remember what the Lord hath done.

Christian   SHAKESPEARE

200

HEAR MY WORDS

Hear my words. Give holy thoughts, and Heaven with gracious love accept my songs, my prayer, my hymn, and preserve me evermore with blessings.

Hindu   *Rig Veda*

201

IMPLANTED CONSCIENCE

When we are children our parents deliver us to the care of a tutor, who is continually to watch over us, that we get no hurt. When we become men, God delivers us to the guardianship of an implanted conscience.

Stoic   EPICTETUS

202

PRAISED BE MY LORD

O most high, almighty, good Lord God,to thee belong praise, glory, honour, and all blessings!

Praised be my Lord God with all his creatures, and specially our brother the sun, who brings us the day and who brings us the light; fair is he and shines with a very great splendour; O Lord, he signifies thee to us!

Praised be my Lord for our sister the moon, and for the stars, the which he has set clear and lovely in the heaven.

Praised be my Lord for our brother the wind, and for air and cloud, calms and all weather, by the which thou upholdest life in all creatures.

Praised be my Lord for our sister water, who is very serviceable to us, and humble and precious and clear.

Praised be my Lord for our brother fire, through whom thou givest light in the darkness, and he is bright and pleasant and very mighty and strong.

Praised be my Lord for our mother the earth, the which doth sustain us and keep us, and bringeth forth divers fruits and flowers and many colours, and grass.

Praised be my Lord for all those who pardon one another for his love's sake, and who endure weakness and tribulation...

Praise ye and bless ye the Lord, and give thanks unto him, and serve him with great humility.

Christian   ST. FRANCIS

203

STRONG IN THY FRIENDSHIP

O God, Lord of power and might!
Strong in Thy friendship, we have no fear.

Hindu   *Rig Veda*

204

ENGRAVEN ON OUR HEARTS

Thy sovereign goodness, Lord of Heaven, is infinite. As a potter Thou hast made all living things. Engraven on our hearts is the sense of Thy goodness. With kindness dost Thou bear with us, and notwithstanding our faults, dost grant us life and prosperity. Let all human beings, all things on earth, rejoice together in Thy great name.

Chinese

205
SONG, DANCE, WORSHIP

Lord, my tongue sings to Thee divine songs. My body dances and worships and turns to Thee. Thou dost not welcome the deserving only; Thou dost not leave out the undeserving. Thou art not vexed with wrongdoers, loving the good only. Blessed be Thou.

Hindu   NAMMALVAR

206
ALL THINGS PRAISE THEE

To celebrate Him, all that thou beholdest is roused to exclamation,
    The heart to understand it becometh an ear;
    Not only is the nightingale on the rose-bush warbling
its hymn of praise,
    But every thorn becometh a tongue to laud His perfection.

Muslim   SADI

207
THE FIVE COLOURS

O friend, I have dyed myself in the colour of my Lord's love.
Have my bodice dipped in the five colours for I am going to
    the dance.
There in the dance my Lord shall meet me—taking off His
    mask.
The moon will perish, the sun will perish and likewise will
    perish the earth and sky.
Wind and water will also perish—but my Lord will remain
    unchanged.

Hindu   MIRA

208

LOVING HEART AND HIDDEN WORDS

Noisy, vain repetitions are an abomination unto Thee, O God. Make us to pray our prayer with loving heart and hidden words, for Thou will do all that is necessary for our daily needs.

Egyptian   *c.* 900 B.C.

209

THOU ART EVERYTHING TO ME

Thou art my Father, and
Thou art my Mother;
Thou art my Kith and Kin, and
Thou art my only Friend.
Thou art my Learning, and
Only Thou art my Wealth.
Thou art the Lord of Lords, and
Thou art Everything to me.
Oh my loving Father
      Lead me from untruth unto truth,
      Lead me from darkness unto light,
      Lead me from death unto deathlessness.
          PEACE, PEACE, PEACE.

Hindu

210

LAUGHTER AND MUSIC

For laughter
God's name be praised;
For cheery companionship,
For old recollections revived
Of labours and joys and dangers gone by.

For humour, the genial good-will,
Of everyday friendship,
God's name be praised.

For music, God's name be praised,
Music that lifts a man's heart from earth
And flings wide the portal of heaven.

And for song,
The gracious flower of perfect song,
God's name be mightily praised.

Christian   JOHN S. HOYLAND

211

THY NAME IS MY HEALING

Thy name is my healing, O my God, and remembrance of Thee is my remedy. Nearness to Thee is my hope, and love for Thee is my companion: Thy mercy to me is my healing and my succour in both this world and the world to come. Thou, verily, art the All-Bountiful, the All-Knowing, the All-Wise.

Bahai   BAHA'U'LLAH

212

THOU AND I

Thou art compassionate
I am forlorn;
Thou givest freely,
I am a beggar in need.

I am known as a sinner,
Thou art known as the Redeemer;
Thou art Protector of the helpless,
Who more helpless than I?
And who can rescue as surely as Thou?

Thou art my Father and my Mother,
My Teacher and my Friend,
Thou art all that I value,
I am bound to Thee in many ways.
Accept me as Thou dost please,
In whatever form,
And grant me the refuge of Thy Feet.

Hindu   TULSI DAS

213

GRATITUDE TO GOD

I cannot draw a breath without gratitude to the Friend, though I know
no gratitude which is worthy of Him.

Every hair of my body is a gift from Him, how express my gratitude
for every hair?

Praise be to the Lord, the giver of all good...

The Wonderful One who created man out of clay, and gave him a
soul, and understanding, and wisdom and a heart...

Since He created thee holy, be thou wise and holy, for it is a shame
to return impure to the earth...

Thou art not able to stand, or set one foot before another, did not
assistance come to thee every moment from the unseen world.

Muslim   SADI

214

NOUGHT IS HEARD BUT PARADISE BIRD

Lord Jesus hath a garden, filled with divers flowers,
Where thou may'st gather posies gay, all times and hours,
      Here nought is heard
      But paradise bird,
      Harp, dulcimer, and lute,
      With cymbal, and timbrel
      And gentle sounding flute.
Oh! Jesus, Lord, my heal and weal, my bliss complete,
Make thou my heart thy garden-plot, true, fair and neat,
      That I may hear
      This music clear,
      Harp, dulcimer, and lute,
      With cymbal, and timbrel
      And gentle sounding flute.

Christian   from the Dutch

215

I HAVE FOUND THE LORD

I have found the Lord who alone was in the beginning, though Himself
beginningless ... I have faith in Thee alone!

Hindu   MIRA

216

PRAISE OF GOD

O Lord,
Thou first didst call us into existence from non-existence . . .
Thou hast led us onward from ignorance to knowledge:
Thou hast shed upon us the light of Thy Book
Thou hast decreed what is to be done, and not done;
But we are ever mingling the evil with the good . . .
We often have lost the way of Thy commandments,
Have often trodden the paths of disobedience;
Yet Thou hast not withdrawn the promise of Thy grace,
Thou hast not hidden from us the light of Thy guidance.

Muslim　　　　　　　　　　　　　　　　　　　　　　　　JAMI

217

GAINING TRUE STRENGTH

No man can be good without Thee. Thou has made the world because Thou art good. As the good never grudges anything good so Thou therefore didst make everything the best possible. Thou has a fatherly mind towards good men, loving them firmly; and letting them be harassed with toils, with pains, with losses, that they may gain true strength.

Stoic　　　　　　　　　　　　　　　　　　　SENECA (adapted)

218

MORE REFRESHING THAN THE MOON

Thou merciful God, there is no giver like thee. How shall I praise thee? I have no words to do it. Thou art kinder than a mother, more refreshing than the moon, thinner than water—all a wave of joy. Thou didst create the nectar, but thou art sweeter than that. Thou art the master of all existence, I lay my head upon thy feet. Forgive me my fault, O God...O God, come and reside in my heart.

Hindu　　　　　　　　　　　　　　　　　　　　　TUKARAMA

219

HIS WRATH IS FINISHED

Though thy servant was disposed to do evil,
Yet is the Lord disposed to be merciful,
The Lord passes not a whole day wroth,
His wrath is finished in a moment, and nought is left.

Egyptian hymn to Amon, *c*. 1300 B.C.

220

THOSE WHO FEAR THEE

Thou, O God, dost deliver those who fear Thee and set them up in a
place of safety; evil shall not touch them neither shall they be grieved.
Thou, O God, art the creator of all things and the governor of all things.
Thou dost hold the keys of heaven and earth.

Muslim *Koran 39.* 61, 62

221

THE GIFT OF SILENCE

For Thy great gift, O Father,
We thank Thee today—
The gift of Silence;
For the rich, warm, generous silence
We thank Thee,
Wherein our souls,
Stunted and shrivelled and starved
In the arid desert of everyday hurry and strain,
May rest, and quietly grow, and expand
Upward to Thee.

Christian JOHN S. HOYLAND

222

OUR GREAT PARENT

God is our Great Parent, do not worry but believe in
Him.

Shinto BUNJIRO

223

GOD, THE ALL-NOURISHER

We cast our seed at the season for sowing,
And leave it when sown to Him, the All-Nourisher;
We look not after the blade of millet or barley,
Till over it hath passed a space of six months;
There is returned to us of all that is sown in our ground
For every seed seven hundred fold.
God is our keeper, and that is enough!
In God is our refuge, and in no one else.

Muslim   NIZAMI

224

YOU ARE DEAR TO ME

Fix your mind on Me, be devoted to Me, worship Me and bow to Me, so shall you without doubt reach Me; This I truly promise to you, for you are dear to Me.

Hindu   *Bhagavad Gita*

225

THOU ART MY LIFE

O Lord, Thou art my life. No other life
Have I· but in and from Thee.
To whom else should I submit but unto Thee?
Thou art the ruler of the Universe. Thou art my life.

Muslim   WILLIAM BASHYR PICKARD

226

I HAVE NO FRIEND BUT GOD

I have no friend but God
Who gave me soul and body and infused me with understanding;
He cherishes and watches over all creatures; He is wise and
    knows the secret of hearts.
The Guru is like a lake; we are his beloved swans:
In the water are many jewels and rubies,
God's praises are pearls, gems and diamonds; singing them
    makes the soul and body happy.

Sikh   GURU NANAK

BRIEF OCCASIONS

. . . Give us this day our daily bread . . .

227

MORNING

a

O Lord our God, the morning is here. Thou who hast chased the slumber from our eyes, and once more assembled us to lift up our hands to Thee in praise, accept our prayers and supplications, and give us faith and love. Bless our going out and coming in, our thoughts, words and works, and let us begin this day with the praise of the unspeakable sweetness of Thy mercy. Hallowed be Thy name, Thy kingdom come. Amen.

Christian   *Greek Church liturgy* (adapted)

b

The dawn light is come, amid all lights and fairest; born is the brilliant far-extending brightness. Night hath yielded a birthplace for the morning.

　　Rich dawn she sets afoot the coiled-up sleeper, one for enjoyment, one for wealth, or worship. All living creatures hath the dawn awakened. Let us arise, the breath, the life, again hath reached us; darkness hath passed away and light approacheth. Singing praises the priest, the poet, rise. Shine then today on him who lauds Thee. Bless the one who offers praise and worship.

Hindu   *Rig Veda*

c

Into thy hands O Lord we commit ourselves this day. Give to each one of us a watchful, a humble, and a diligent spirit, that we may seek in all things to know thy will, and when we know it may perform it perfectly and gladly, to the honour and glory of thy name.

Christian   *Gelasian Sacramentary*

d

When a man has learnt wisdom in the morning he may be content to die in the evening before the sun sets.

Confucian

e

Grant us,O Lord, to pass this day in gladness and peace, without stumbling and without stain, that reaching the eventide victorious over all temptation, we may praise thee, the eternal God, who art blessed, and dost govern all things, world without end. Amen.

Christian   *Mozarabic Liturgy*

f

The dawn called the Muezzin to the first prayer,
PRAISE BE TO GOD, THE EVER LIVING AND THE NEVER DYING!
And the morn of felicity dawned upon me
And I awoke to new life with the morning breeze.

Muslim   NIZAMI

g

O wonderful!
The sun arises, and all the world is lighted.
    So wakes the mind to truth, and man, benighted in error, sees its brightness, and adores.

Buddhist   *Avatamsaka Sutra*

h

All that is in the heavens and in the earth glorifieth God (Allah) ...
He causes the night to pass into the day, and He causes the day to pass into the night, and He·is knower of all that is.

Muslim   *Koran 57.1,6*

i

Brother, the day hath broken,
Awake,
Remember thy God.

Hindu   *Sahajram*

j

When the sun rises up then the earth, made by God (Ahura) becomes clean; the running waters become clean, the waters of the wells become clean, the waters of the sea become clean, the standing waters become clean; all the holy creatures, the creatures of the Good Spirit, become clean.

Zoroastrian   *Zend-Avesta*

k

O friend, awake, and sleep no more! The night is over and gone, would you lose your day also?

Hindu   KABIR

l

Awake, O man, now is the break of day.
Thy life is running out like water from thy palm.
The bell ringeth out each hour; the day that hath passed
    will not return.
The sun and moon warm thee; thy life is drawing every
    day nearer to its end.
Know Ram (God) within thyself. Utter Ram's name alone,
    and see Him by deep meditation.

Hindu   DADU

228

END OF THE DAY

a

O kind Father, loving Father, through Thy mercy we have spent our day in peace and happiness; grant that we may, according to Thy will, do what is right.

Give us light, give us understanding, so that we may know what pleases Thee.

We offer this prayer in Thy presence, O wonderful Lord:

Forgive us our sins. Help us in keeping ourselves pure. Bring us into the fellowship of those in whose company we may remember Thy name.

(Through Nanak) may Thy Name forever be on the increase, and may all men prosper by Thy grace.

Sikh   GURU GOBIND SINGH

b

Grant us Thy peace upon our homeward way; with Thee began, with Thee shall end the day; guard Thou the lips from sin, the hearts from shame, that in this place have called upon Thy name.

Grant us Thy peace, Lord, through the coming night; turn Thou for us its darkness into light; from harm and danger keep Thy children free, for dark and light are both alike to Thee.

Grant us Thy peace throughout our earthly life, our balm in sorrow and our stay in strife; then, when Thy voice shall bid our conflicts cease, call us, O Lord, to Thine eternal peace.

Christian   JOHN ELLERTON

229

NIGHT

a

Take us we pray thee, O Lord of our life, into thy keeping this night and for ever. O thou Light of Lights, keep us from inward darkness. Grant us so to sleep in peace that we may arise to work according to thy will.

Christian   BISHOP ANDREWS

b

So favour us this night, O Thou whose pathways we have visited as birds who nest upon the tree. Night hath put all her glories on; the villagers have sought their homes, and all that walks and all that flies. Keep wolf and thief away; from falling lightnings keep us safe great King of all the mighty world.

Hindu   *Rig Veda 10*

c

O Lord God refresh us with quiet sleep when we are wearied with the day's labour, that, being assisted with the help which our weakness needs, we may be devoted to thee both in body and mind, through Jesus Christ our Lord.

Christian   *Leonine Sacramentary*

d

Glory be to God (Allah) when ye enter the night and when ye enter the morning. Unto Him be praises in the heavens and the earth, and at the sun's decline and in the noonday.

Muslim   *Koran 30.*17

230

THE NEW YEAR

a

O God of time and eternity, who makest us creatures of time, to the end that when time is over we may attain to thy blessed eternity. With time, which is thy gift, give us also wisdom to redeem the time lest our day of grace be lost.

Christian   CHRISTINA G. ROSSETTI

b

Another year is dawning; dear Master, let it be, in working or in waiting, another year with thee.

Another year of progress, another year of praise, another year of proving thy presence all the days.

Another year is dawning; dear Master, let it be, on earth, or else in heaven, another year for thee.

Christian   FRANCES R. HAVERGAL

c

Thanks to Him whose Truth abides in you,
Thanks to Him who thus is born within you.
May every year beginning, and every end of time
Be His birthday for you.

Hindu   *Vedas*

231

THE LAND WE LOVE THE MOST

a

Lord, while for all mankind we pray, of every clime and coast, O hear us for our native land, the land we love the most.

O guard our shores from every foe; with peace our borders bless; with prosperous times our cities crown, our fields with plenteousness.

Unite us in the sacred love of knowledge, truth, and thee; and let our hills and valleys shout the songs of liberty.

Lord of the nations, thus to thee our country we commend; be thou her refuge and her trust, her everlasting friend.

Christian   JOHN REYNELL WREFORD

b

Lord, who hast given us this land for our abiding place, help us to love it with a passion so strong and true that we may be jealous of its honour and instant in its service. So work through us that it may become a land where men walk in the freedom of the truth and in the light of knowledge, and where industry shall go hand in hand with joy.

Christian   *Inner Light*

c

God bless our native land: may thy protecting hand still guard our shore. May peace her power extend, foe be transformed to friend, and Britain's rights depend on war no more!

Nor on this land alone: but be God's mercies known from shore to shore! And may the nations see that men should brothers be, and form one family the wide world o'er.

Christian   W.E. HICKSON

232

SCRIPTURES

a

When quiet in my house I sit,
   Thy Book be my companion still,
My joy thy sayings to repeat,

Talk o'er the records of thy will,
And search the oracles divine,
Till every heartfelt word be mine.

Christian   CHARLES WESLEY

b

Let the scriptures be our authority in determining what ought to be done or what ought not to be done, knowing that what has been declared by the ordinances of scriptures we ought to work in this world.

Hindu   *Bhagavad Gita*

c

Blessed Lord, by whose providence all Holy Scriptures were written and preserved for our instruction: give us grace to study them each day with patience and love; strengthen our souls with the fullness of their divine teaching; keep from us all pride and irreverence; guide us in the deep things of thy heavenly wisdom; and, of thy great mercy, lead us by thy Word into everlasting life.

Christian   BISHOP WESTCOTT

d

O ye people of the Scripture! Now hath our messenger come unto you, expounding unto you the Scripture. Now hath come unto you light from God and a plain Scripture.

Muslim   *Koran 5. 15*

233

PRAYER PREPARATION

He whose mind is not quietened cannot pray.

Jewish   *Talmud*

234

GATHERED HERE TOGETHER

a

O Thou kind Lord! These are Thy servants here gathered, turned towards Thy kingdom and in need of Thy blessings. O God, we are ignorant; make us wise. We are dead; make us alive. We are material; endow us with spirit. O God, resuscitate us, give us sight, give us hearing. Familiarize us with the mysteries of life, so that the secrets of Thy kingdom may become revealed to us. Thou are mighty! Thou art powerful! Thou art the Giver and Thou art the Ever-Bounteous!

Bahai   ABDU'L-BAHA

b

O Lord, we beseech thee to bless and prosper us, gathered here together this day. Grant us reasonableness in all our dealings with each other. Make us large-hearted in helping and generous in criticizing. Keep us from unkind words and unkind silence. Make us quick to understand the needs and feelings of others, and grant that, living in the brightness of thy presence, we may bring thy sunshine into cloudy places, like true followers of Jesus Christ, our Lord.

Christian   S.G.H.

c

O God, give us sincerity here now in worship. Help us, by the light of thy presence, to see the sin in ourselves and truly repent of it. And as we declare humbly our longing for deep faith, strengthen our belief and lead us into rich communion with thee. And may our lives increasingly show forth thy praise.

Christian   S.G.H.

235

LET THE PEOPLE ATTEND

Let not the Church be rent in twain by any person, and let the people attend the services each fast day.

Buddhist   ASOKA

236

EDUCATION

We are so ignorant, O God, and there is so much to learn. Whichever way we look these are things beyond our present powers and which as yet we have had no time to study. Strengthen us that while education is still so easily available to us we waste no opportunity to get it, that in the future we may be more useful to others, and to thee.

Christian   S.G.H.

237

CAREER CHOICE

O God, give us wisdom and understanding when we come to make choice of career or employment, that may have so much to do with the happiness and usefulness of our lives. May there be work for us to do. Show us where our talents lie and may we not be hasty, nor influenced by quick material gain. But, waiting on thee, may we feel thy sure guidance.

Christian   S.G.H.

238

MEMBERS LEAVING

Bless, O God, those who are going from here to begin a new life elsewhere. May what they have learned with us help them on their way; may grateful memories strengthen them; may friendships cheer them, and may they with unflagging courage serve thee in the world and follow with us our Lord, Christ Jesus.

Christian   S.G.H.

239

TRAVELLERS

O God, who didst call Abraham to leave his home, and didst protect him in all his wanderings, grant to those who now travel by land, sea, or air, a prosperous journey, a quiet time, and a safe arrival at their journey's end. Be to them a shadow in the heat, a refuge in the tempest, a protection in adversity, and grant that when life's pilgrimage is over, they may arrive at the heavenly country.

Christian   *Priest's Prayer Book*

240

FOR ONE WHO IS SICK

O Lord, in the greatness of thy love, look upon our friend in *his (her)* sickness. Bless the means used for *his* recovery, and strengthen all who tenderly care for *him.* Give *him,* we pray thee, comfort and sure confidence in thee. Lift up the light of thy countenance upon *him* and give *him* peace.

Christian   *About the Feet of God*

241

FOR THE AGED

O Lord Jesus Christ, who didst hearken unto the prayer of thy two disciples and abide with them, when it was toward evening and the day was far spent: abide, we pray thee, with thine aged servants in the evening of life. Make thyself known unto them and whensoever they shall pass through the valley of the shadow of death, be with them unto the end.

Christian

242

DEATH

a

When I go from hence let this be my parting word, that what I have seen is unsurpassable.

I have tasted of the hidden honey of this lotus that expands on the ocean of light, and thus am I blessed—let this be my parting word.

In this playhouse of infinite forms I have had my play and here have I caught sight of him that is formless.

My whole body and my limbs have been thrilled with his touch who is beyond touch; and if the end comes here—let this be my parting word.

Hindu   TAGORE, *Gitanjali*

b

O God, when we try to obliterate the frontier of clouds which separates us from the other world, guide our unpractised movements. And, when the given hour shall strike, arouse us, eager as the traveller who straps on his rucksack while beyond the misty window-pane the earliest rays of dawn are faintly visible.

Christian   GABRIEL MARCEL

c

Death is not extinguishing the light, it is only putting out the lamp because the dawn has come.

Hindu   TAGORE

d

Sunset and evening star,
    And one clear call for me!
And may there be no moaning at the bar,
    When I put out to sea,
But such a tide as moving seems asleep,
    Too full for sound and foam,
When that which drew from out the boundless deep
    Turns again home.

Twilight and evening bell,
    And after that the dark!
And may there be no sadness of farewell
    When I embark;
For though from out our bourne of time and space
    The flood may bear me far,
I hope to see my Pilot face to face
    When I have crost the bar.

Christian   TENNYSON

e

I have got my leave. Bid me farewell, my brothers. I bow to you all
and take my departure . . . .

We were neighbours for long, but I received more than I could give.
Now the day has dawned and the lamp that lit my dark corner is out. A
summons has come and I am ready for my journey.

Hindu   TAGORE, *Gitanjali*

f

So he passed over and all the trumpets sounded for him on the other
side.

Christian   BUNYAN, *Pilgrim's Progress*

g

In the Name of God (Allah), the Merciful, the Compassionate:
   Whoever is sincere in his devotion will expose his life;
whoever is timid is but a lover of himself.

   Death on a sudden draweth me into his ambush; how much
better that I fall into the snares of my Beloved One!

   Since without doubt death is written on my brow, death will
be the sweeter by the hand of the Comforter.

   Wilt thou not one day helplessly surrender thy soul?
Better then is it that thou shouldst surrender it at the feet
   of one who loveth thee.

Muslim   SADI

h

I know not what the future hath
   Of marvel or surprise,
Assured alone that life or death
   His mercy underlies.

And so beside the silent sea
   I wait the muffled oar;
No harm from Him can come to me
   On ocean or on shore.

I know not where His islands lift
 Their fronded palms in air;
I only know I cannot drift
 Beyond His love and care.

Christian   JOHN GREEENLEAF WHITTIER

243

VIRTUE LIVES ON

In word, in act, be justice in our view:
Nor ever any thoughtless course pursue:
And this good truth bear always in our mind
That once to die is destined for mankind.
And while wealth fails one lasting joy to give,
The gifts of virtue shall for ever live.

Greek   PYTHAGORAS

244

AWAKENING INTO HEAVEN

Bring us, O Lord God, at our last awakening into the house and gate of heaven, to enter into that gate and dwell in that house, where there shall be no darkness nor dazzling, but one equal light; no noise nor silence, but one equal music; no fears nor hopes, but one equal possession; no ends nor beginnings, but one equal eternity; in the habitations of thy majesty and thy glory, world without end.

Christian   JOHN DONNE

245

THE JUST SOUL ENTERS HEAVEN

O Most Holy One! Creator of the Worlds!
When that a man is dead, where dwells his Soul?
And where, O Lord, doth retribution come
To meet him, whatso'er of good or ill
He may have drawn upon him in this world
Corporeal? Speak, O Thou Most Holy Lord! . . .

... across the mountains high
Unto the Holy Bridge by God created
Till they reach the Gate of Paradise,
His own good Thoughts, good Words, and holy Deeds
Lead on the Soul ... the just man's soul steps forth
And entereth the immortal Home of God.

Zoroastrian   L. C. CASARTELLI

246

FOR PARLIAMENT AND RULERS

Grant and continue unto us a succession of legislators and rulers who have been taught the wisdom of the Kingdom of God.

Endow all members of Parliament with a right understanding, a pure purpose and sound speech; enable them to rise above all self-seeking and party zeal into the larger sentiments of public good and human brotherhood. Purge our political life of every evil; subdue in the nation all unhallowed thirst for conquest or vain glory. Inspire us with calmness and self-restraint, and the endeavour to get thy will done everywhere upon the earth.

Christian   JOHN HUNTER

247

IN TIMES OF NATIONAL DIFFICULTY

O Holy Spirit of God, guide, we pray thee, all those to whom thou hast committed special responsibility at this time. Give them wisdom and understanding, discernment and self-control that they may uphold what is right and perform what is just, so that in all things thy will be done.

Christian   *Uppingham School Prayers*

248

FOR A PARTICULAR OCCASION OR AFFAIR

O God, I desire thy blessing by Thy knowledge, and I beg of Thee to give me power to do it, and I ask of Thee Thy great grace, for Thou hast the power while I have not, and Thou knowest while I do not, and Thou art the Great Knower of the unseen things, O God! If Thou knowest that this affair is good for me in the matter of my religion and my living, then ordain it for me and make it easy for me and bless me therein; and if Thou knowest that this affair is evil for me in the matter of my religion and my living, then turn it away from me and turn me away from it and ordain what is good for me wheresoever it is, and make me contented with it.

Muslim   MUHAMMAD

249

OUR AMUSEMENTS AND RECREATIONS

Grant, O Lord, that we may carry the true spirit of joy into our amusements and recreations, whatever they may be. Grant that we may not be dependent on them for our only means of happiness, nor let them blot out from our minds the thought of thee. Help us to find thee and thy joy in all these good things, that they may fit us to serve thee better.

Christian   DIANA PONSONBY

250

OUR FRIENDS THE ANIMALS

a

Hear our humble prayer, O God, for our friends the animals, especially for animals who are suffering; for all that are overworked and underfed and cruelly treated; for all wistful creatures in captivity that beat against their bars; for any that are hunted or lost or deserted or frightened or hungry; for all that are in pain or dying; for all that must be put to death. We entreat for them all mercy and pity, and for those who deal with them we ask a heart of compassion and gentle hands and kindly words. Make us ourselves to be true friends to animals and so to share the blessings of the merciful.

Christian   RUSSIAN PRAYER

b

For those, O Lord, the humble beasts, that bear with us the burden and heat of the day, and offer their guileless love for the well being of their countries: we supplicate Thy tenderness of heart, for Thou hast promised to save both man and beast, and great is Thy loving kindness, O Master, Saviour of the world.

Christian   EASTERN CHURCH

c

We beseech thee, O Lord, to hear our supplications on behalf of the dumb creation, who after their kind, bless, praise, and magnify thee for ever. Grant that all cruelty may cease in our land, and deepen our thankfulness to thee for the faithful companionship of those whom we delight to call our friends.

Christian   R.S.P.C.A.

251

IN PERIL ON THE SEA

Eternal Father, strong to save,
Whose arm doth bind the restless wave,
Who bidd'st the mighty ocean deep
Its own appointed limits keep,
O hear us when we cry to Thee
For those in peril on the sea.

Christian   WILLIAM WHITING

252

ON SEEING THE RAINBOW

Blessed art thou, O Lord our God, King of the Universe who rememberest the covenant and art faithful to thy covenant and keepest thy promise.

Jewish   *Prayer Book*

253

AGAINST ANGER

O Jesu, calm me!

Christian   E. B. PUSEY

254

ON SEEING TREES BLOSSOMING

Blessed art thou, O Lord our King. King of the Universe, who hast made thy world lacking in nought, but hast produced therein goodly creatures and goodly trees wherewith to give delight unto the children of men.

Jewish   *Prayer Book*

255

THY FROST AND SNOW

Almighty God, who rulest the changing seasons, and fulfillest in all thine own unchanging purpose: we bless thee that beneath all that now in winter seems cold and dead, thou art keeping safe the hidden germs of life, and preparing for the days when the earth shall again bud and blossom, and bring forth her harvest. And still dost thou clothe all things around us with the perfection of beauty, sending forth thy frost and snow, filling the brief day with sunshine, and making the night glorious with countless stars. We thank thee for the shelter and comfort of our homes, and pray for the kind and compassionate heart toward all whose lot is harder and who in poverty or sickness shrink before the cold.

Christian   JOHN HUNTER

256

ON DUTY

Hour by hour resolve firmly, like a Roman and a man, to do what comes to hand with correct and natural dignity, and with humanity, independence and justice. . . . This you can do if you will approach each action as if it were your last, dismissing the wayward thought, the emotional recoil from the commands of reason, the desire to create an impression, the admiration of self, the discontent with your lot. See how little a man needs to master, for his days to flow on in quietness and piety; he has but to observe these few counsels, and God will ask nothing more.

Stoic MARCUS AURELIUS

257
GOSSIP

Lord, remind us often that a gossip's mouth is the
devil's mailbag.

Christian Welsh proverb

258
OUR BODIES AND MINDS

O God, may we so value our bodies and minds that we never mar them. May we not be tricked into bad habits by publicity and advertisements that deliberately mislead, or by the desire for easy applause, or by the fear of being thought narrow. But may we be sturdy and upright in our thinking and our behaviour, and treat our bodies as the temple of thy Spirit. And may we remember also the influence of our example on those who may be weaker than ourselves.

Christian S.G.H.

259
AT ALL TIMES

For thinking upon God no separate time is required,
It should go on at all times.
Learn to place your affections on the highest,
All else that is spread out is vain.

Hindu TUKARAMA

260
GRACES FOR FOOD

a

Eat of the things provided, and render thanks to God (Allah).

Muslim *Koran 2.* 172

b

Benedictus benedicat, per Iesum Christum, dominum nostrum. (Let him that is blessed give glessing, through Jesus Christ, our Lord.)
Christian

c

We worship God (Ahura Mazda) who created the cattle, and the waters, and the wholesome plants.

Zoroastrian   *Zend-Avesta*

d

For what we are about to receive may the Lord make us truly thankful.
Christian

e

Thou Thyself art the Giver; Thou art the Enjoyer; I know none beside Thee.
Sikh

f

Whatever thou doest or eatest, do that as dedicated to Me.

Hindu   *Bhagavad Gita*

g

To take all one wants is never so good as to stop when one should.

Taoist   *Tao Te Ching*

h

Blessed art Thou, O Lord our God, King of the universe, who createst many living beings with their wants, for all the means Thou hast created to sustain the life of each of them. Blessed be he who is the life of all worlds.

Jewish   *Prayer Book*

261

CLOSING BENEDICTIONS

a

The splendour, the love, and the strength of God be upon us.

Christian   C.S. LEWIS, *Perelandra*

b

Praise be unto God, the Lord of Glory, and peace be upon his people.

Muslim

c

O Great Creator, inspirer of good thoughts within our souls, the prayers of our understanding seek for Thee. To Thee, O God (Ahura Mazda), we ascribe all good.

Zoroastrian   *Zend-Avesta* (adapted)

d

Thine, O Lord, is the greatness, and the power, and the glory, and the victory, and the majesty; for all that is in the heaven and in the earth is thine.

Jewish   *Old Testament*

e

O God, the Peaceful, the Good, the One, bring us into thy Truth and Peace.

Hindu   *Upanishads*

f

Gratia Domini nostri Iesu Christi cum spiritu vestro. Amen. (The grace of our Lord Jesus Christ be with you all. Amen.)

Christian   *Revelation 22*

g

Let us be at peace in this world and happy in the next, because God has taken us unto himself.

Sikh   *Sukhmanu* (adapted)

h

May Enlightenment arise within us—a moon of thought to cool the fever of sin, a great sun driving away the gloom of ignorance. So may wake our mind to Truth.

Buddhist   (adapted)

i

May we free ourselves from doubt, open and behold the great broad Way of Truth, and find our lives quickened in the midst of the goodness of God.

Shinto

j

Thou who art One in Many, Many in One, yet neither One nor Many—we bow to Thee.

Jain   (adapted)

k

May our minds be released and free and unclinging to all things of the earth.

Zen

l

Remember the name of thy Lord and devote thyself with a complete devotion. Lord of the East and West; there is no God save him.

Muslim   *Koran 73.* 8,9

m

May we rest our mind on the God that is beyond time, hard to be seen, dwelling in the mystery of things and in the heart of man, and rejoice with much joy.

Hindu   *Katha Upanishad* (adapted)

n

Offer yourselves as a sacrifice to the all-pervading Deity. Let this be your law of life—meditate on the name of God.

Sikh   GURU RAM DAS

o

May the grace of love, courage, gaiety, and the quiet mind, which is the grace of the Lord Jesus, be with us now and always.

Christian   ROBERT LOUIS STEVENSON (adapted)

p

Freed from joy and sorrow may we find our true selves and dwell for evermore in the wondrous realm of God.

Sufi   ABDULLAH ANSARI (adapted)

q

May we all remain fast and firm in faith, that the glory of glories may rest upon us. Thou art the Gracious, the Bountiful, the Merciful, the Compassionate.

Bahai   ABDU'L-BAHA (adapted)

r

Glory to Thee, glory to Thee, O Lord, O Lord of the Universe, O Sovereign God: Glory to Thee, O Creator. Glory to Thee, O Holy God.

Hindu   DADU

INTERCESSION

. . . and forgive us our trespasses . . .

262

MY TONGUE AND EVIL

O God guard my tongue from evil and my lips from speaking deceitfully. To those who wrong me may my soul be silent; yet let me be humble as the dust to everyone. Open thou my heart to thy will; strengthen my desire to obey thy commandments. May my thoughts and my prayers be acceptable unto thee now and evermore.

Jewish   *Talmud*

263

MY BOAT IS SO SMALL

Protegez-moi, mon Seigneur; mon navire est si petit, et votre mer est si grande.

   (Protect me, my Lord, my boat is so small, and your ocean so big.)

Christian   Breton Fishermen's prayer

264

CRY OF THE FISHERS

'Dear Lord, thy sea is great—our boats are small!'
So cry the fishers of the Northern sea
When God's high wind ariseth stormily,
Uplifting them before a sudden fall.
Thus in distress we also oftimes call
When blindly beaten to and fro are we,
Far from the haven where we fain would be.
While wind-swept seas our melting hearts appal,
And when for us the waves thereof are still
And we would gladly help those storm-tossed souls
Who yet are struggling 'neath the tempest's weight;
Feeling the frailty of all human skill.
We humbly whisper while the thunder rolls,
'Dear Lord, our boats are small—thy sea is great!'

Christian   ELLEN THORNEYCROFT FOWLER

265

THE RIGHT WAY

May we, O God, keep ourselves modest, faithful, and
valiant. Show us the way and keep us in it.

Stoic   EPICTETUS

266

THY HOLY PRESENCE

O Eternal Light, shine into our hearts;
Eternal Goodness, deliver us from evil;
Eternal Power, be thou our support;
Eternal Wisdom, scatter our ignorance;
Eternal Pity, have mercy upon us.
Grant that with all our heart, and mind, and strength, we
    may evermore seek thy face; and finally bring us by thine
    infinite mercy, to thy holy presence.

Christian   ALCUIN

267

CHANGE ME

O Thou that changest earth into gold,
And out of other earth madest the father of mankind . . .
Change my mistakes and forgetfulness to knowledge;
I am altogether vile, make me temperate and meek.

Sufi   JELALEDDIN RUMI

268

CROWNED WITH THORNS

Take away out of our hearts, O Lord God, all self-confidence and
boasting, all high and vain thoughts, all desire to excuse ourselves for
our sins or to compare ourselves proudly with others; and grant us
rather to take as master and King him who chose to be crowned with
thorns and to die in shame for others and for us all, thy Son our
Saviour Jesus Christ.

Christian   DEAN VAUGHAN

269

ACTION AND INACTION

May we sow kindly acts, and reap their fruition, being sure that inaction in a deed of mercy becomes an action of deadly sin.

Buddhist   *Metta Sutta*

270

GOOD DEEDS

O God, grant me this boon,
Never should I turn away from good deeds;
Nor when fighting adversity should I be afraid,
But with a firm resolve, should I achieve victory;
Over my heart should I have complete control.
O Lord, that is what I crave of Thy Name.
When finally time comes for me to rest,
Let me die in the thick of these battles.

Sikh   GURU GOBIND SINGH

271

DANGERS AND TRIALS

Grant, O Lord, that we may carefully watch over our tempers and every unholy feeling. Remove whatever in us may be a stumbling block in another's way; that, by conforming to thy will in small things, we may hope by thy protection and help to pass safely through the greater dangers and trials to which we may be exposed;

Christian   CHRISTINA ROSSETTI

272

IN TIME OF DISTRESS

With all my heart I am come to you for protection—
With body, and voice, and mind, O God.
Nothing else is admitted to my thoughts—
My desire remains fixed on you,
There is a heavy load on me,
Except you, who will remove it, O God.

Hindu   TUKARAMA

273

IN THE HEREAFTER

Our Lord, grant us good in this world, and good in the Hereafter, and save us from the chastisement of the Fire.

Muslim   *Koran 2.* 201

274

WHAT WE NEED

Lord we know not what we ought to ask of thee; thou only knowest what we need; thou lovest us better than we know how to love ourselves. O Father, give to us, thy children, that which we ourselves know not how to ask. We would have no other desire than to accomplish thy will. Teach us to pray, and pray thyself in us.

Christian   FENELON

275

THE GOOD FIGHT

O Force divine, supreme illuminator, listen to our prayer, do not go far from us, do not withdraw, help us to fight the good fight, fortify our strength for the struggle, give us the power for victory!

O my sweet Master, marvellous Unknowable, Dispenser of all boons, Thou who bringest light to birth out of darkness and force out of weakness, support our efforts, guide our steps, lead us to victory.

Hindu   SRI AUROBINDO

276

THE NAKED BRANCH

Dost thou not behold the tree in the winterly season, how it standeth leafless in the piercing cold?

See how it holdeth out its hands in supplication.

Like the naked branch, let us lift up our hands.

O Lord, do Thou look upon us benignantly, that our sins may be removed. Let us have mercy from Thee who art the Pardoner of transgressors. Greatness or meanness assign us, and it is enough . . .

Do Thou uphold me, and no one else shall cast me down.

Muslim   SADI

277

THESE DAYS OF OUR YOUTH

O Lord Jesus, Saviour of mankind, who hast taught us that to gain the whole world and lose our own soul is a folly of everlasting consequence, through thy eternal wisdom help us in these days of our youth when ambition, pleasure, and searching temptation knock loud at the door. We would all make the choice that is right, the choice that would have been thine. Watch with us, therefore, when we shut the doors of the heart against the world and its discordant voices, to make the far-reaching decisions of life. May we not shame thee there in our most secret resolves. And in the lesser acts of life, teach us, O Lord, that nothing is too slight to be important. If we have tampered with honour or conscience, even made foolish boasts of our dishonour, have mercy upon us and reveal the truer way of life.

Christian   CONRAD SKINNER

278

THE DIVINE GURU

I come to take refuge with the Lord;
    May the Divine Guru out of His mercy grant that the passions of lust, anger, greed, pride and undue attachment in me may vanish and leave me in peace.

Sikh   *Sukhmanu 6*

279

GOD'S PRESENCE AND GUIDANCE

Grant, O Lord God, that we may utterly believe in thy presence;
    That we may wait, reverently and anxiously, as servants standing in the presence of their Lord, for the slightest sign or hint of thy will;
    That we may welcome all truth, under whatever outward forms it be uttered;
    That we may have grace to receive new thought with grace—gracefully, courteously, fairly, charitably, reverently;
    That we may believe firmly that, however strange or startling, it may come from Thee whose ways are not as our ways or thoughts as our thoughts;

That we may bless every good deed, by whomsoever it be done;

That we may rise above all party strife and cries, all party fashions and shibboleths, to the contemplation of thy Eternal Truth and Goodness, O God Almighty who never changest.

Christian CHARLES KINGSLEY

280

THOU WHO ART POWER

Thou who art Power fill me with power.
Thou who art Valour infuse valour into me.
Thou who art Strength give me strength.
Thou who art the Vital Essence endow me with vitality.
Thou who art Wrath against wrong instil that wrath into me.
Thou who art Fortitude fill me with fortitude.

Hindu *Yajur Veda*

281

THE LOVE OF GOODNESS FIRST

Almighty and most merciful God, we acknowledge and confess that we have sinned against thee in thought, and word, and deed; that we have not loved thee with all our heart and soul, with all our mind and strength; and that we have not loved our neighbour as ourselves. We beseech thee, O God, to be forgiving to what we have been, to help us to amend what we are, and of thy mercy to direct what we shall be, so that the love of goodness may ever be first in our hearts, and we may follow unto our life's end in the steps of Jesus Christ our Lord.

Christian JOHN HUNTER

282

LET NOT OUR MIND

Our eyes may see some uncleanness, but let not our mind see things that are not clean. Our ears may hear some uncleanness, but let not our mind hear things that are not clean.

Shinto

283

THY GREAT PURPOSE

O my God! Unite the hearts of Thy servants and reveal to them Thy
Great Purpose. May they follow Thy Commandments and abide in Thy
Law. Help them, O God, in their endeavour, and grant them strength to
serve Thee. O God leave them not to themselves, but guide their steps
by the light of Thy knowledge and cheer their hearts by Thy love,
Verily, Thou art their Helper and their Lord.

Bahai   BAHA'U'LLAH

284

OM!

OM!
    Oh, Thou Perfectly Enlightened, enlighten all sentient
      beings!
    Oh, Thou who art perfect in wisdom and compassion,
      emancipate all beings, and bring them to Buddhahood.

Zen   (*OM, see 33)

285

THE HEARTS OF MYSTICS

O God, seek me out of thy mercy that I may come to Thee; and draw
me on with thy grace that I may turn to thee.
    O thou who art veiled in the shrouds of thy glory, so that no eye can
perceive thee! O thou, who shinest forth in the perfection of thy
splendour so that only the hearts of mystics have realized thy majesty!
How shalt thou be hidden, seeing that thou art ever manifest; or how
shalt thou be absent, seeing that thou art ever present and watchest
over us.

Sufi   IBN ATA ALLAH

286

A POET'S PRAYER

Thou it is who hast prepared the materials for my labour . . .
It is Thy liberality which hath kindly accepted my service,
And whose grace hath exalted me from the prostration of devotion,

Through Thee I have rubbed my forehead in the dust of Thy ways . . .
Thou hast given to my tongue the power of praise,
Thou hast touched my heart with the memory of Thy goodness,
Thou hast tipped my tongue with richness and sweetness . . .
Let not my tongue to run into evil-speaking.

Muslim   JAMI

287

ANCIENT GIFTS

Grant us, O Lord, these ancient gifts:

Give to us Wisdom, that is more precious than rubies, guiding our consciences so that we may distinguish what is right and what is wrong.

Give to us a strong sense of Duty so that we know when to be strict and unyielding with ourselves.

Give us the royal gift of Courage so that we may dare to do right whatever the consequences.

Give to us a keen sense of Honour, that we may readily admit our own faults; sternly oppose all that is not pure and honourable, and be just and generous to those we dislike.

Give to us worthy Ambition that we may fit ourselves to serve others and to use to the full all the high powers we possess.

Give to us a sense of Humour, that we may be saved from being pompous or priggish, and made able not only to laugh with others but at ourselves.

Grant us these ancient gifts, O Lord, we pray.

Christian   adapted S.G.H.

288

TRUTH

May we ever follow the path of truthfulness, for Truth belongs to thy Good Spirit and Falsehood to the Evil Spirit. Let us choose always Truth, and try to put down Falsehood.

Zoroastrian

289

THE RIGHT BLESSINGS

O Lord our God, teach us, we beseech thee, to ask thee aright for the right blessings. Steer thou the vessel of our life towards thyself, thou tranquil haven of all storm-tossed souls. Show us the course wherein we should go. Renew a willing spirit within us. Let thy spirit curb our wayward senses, and guide us into that which is our true good, to keep thy laws, and in all our works evermore to rejoice in thy glorious and gladdening presence. For thine is the glory and praise from all thy saints, for ever and ever.

Christian   ST. BASIL

290

FOR THAT ART THOU

O Thou, sole Reality, Light of our light and Life of our life, Love supreme, Saviour of the world, grant that more and more I may be perfectly awakened to the awareness of thy constant presence. Let all my acts conform to Thy law; let there be no difference between my will and Thine. Extricate me from the illusory consciousness of my mind, from its world of phantasies; let me identify my consciousness with the Absolute Consciousness, for that art Thou.

Hindu   SRI AUROBINDO

291

GIVE EAR, O GOD

Give ear unto my prayer, O God, and hide not thyself from my supplication.

Jewish   *Psalm 55*

292

EVIL TAKE AWAY

Blest Saviour, changeless light of man,
Of all the hope and stay,
Give good things unto those that need,
And evil take away.

Christian   *Christian Epigrams*, from Greek anthology

293

LEST WE LOSE HEART

O gracious Lord, with whom disguise is vain,
Mask not our evil, let us see it plain!
But veil the weakness of our good desire,
Lest we lose heart and falter and expire.

Sufi   JELALEDDIN RUMI

294

ABLE TO GUIDE US

Let us not think in our heart that God is forgetful of
us. Let us give ourselves to Him for He is able to guide us.
   O Glorious God, guide my eyes that they look no evil look.
   Guide my ears that they hear no evil word.
   Guide my mouth that it utter no slander.
   Guide for me my hands that they serve not Satan.
   Guide for me my heart that it do no evil at all.
   Guide for me my Spirit in the midst of the stormy sea.
   Guide my feet that they walk not in the way of Error.
   Glory and honour to Jesus, the King of the Holy Ones.

Manichaean   *Psalms*

295

PEACE, LIFE, WISDOM

O God, may we live in Peace one with another, and may thy Peace,
Life, and Wisdom rule us all.

Christian   GEORGE FOX (adapted)

296

ONE PIECE OF IRON

O Lord, don't count my faults. You make no distinction between
sinner and saint. Consider me as your own.
   One piece of iron is kept in the temple, and another piece used as a
butcher's knife, but the philosopher's stone would turn either into gold,
so, O Lord, you are like the philosopher's stone which does not make
distinction.

One water stream is called a drain, the other a river, but the moment they merge in the Ganges they become Ganges. So You are like the Ganges.

Hindu   SURDAS

297

EARTH'S SIN AND STRIFE

Almighty Father, who dost give the gift of life to all who live, look down on all earth's sin and strife, and lift us to a nobler life.

Lift up our hearts, O King of kings, to brighter hopes and kindlier things; to visions of a larger good, and holier dreams of brotherhood.

The world is weary of its pain, of selfish greed and fruitless gain, of tarnished honour, falsely strong, and all its ancient deeds of wrong.

Hear thou the prayer thy servants pray, uprising from all lands today, and o'er the vanquished powers of sin, O bring thy great salvation in.

Christian   JOHN H. B. MASTERMAN

298

THE FACE OF TRUTH

The face of Truth is covered with a golden veil. Unveil it, O God of Light, that we who love the true may behold its glory.

Hindu   *Upanishads*

299

FAITH WITHOUT FEAR

Give us a faith which makes us friends of Thee, O God, not a faith that makes us afraid. In faith may we come near to Thee.

Shinto   BUNJIRO

300

OUR WANDERING FOOTSTEPS GUIDE

O God of Bethel by whose hand thy people still are fed; who through this earthly pilgrimage hast all our fathers led—

Our vows, our prayers, we now present before thy throne of grace; God of our fathers, be the God of their succeeding race.

Through each perplexing path of life our wandering footsteps guide; give us each day our daily bread and raiment fit provide.

O spread thy covering wings around till all our wanderings cease, and at our Father's loved abode our souls arrive in peace.

Christian   PHILIP DODDRIDGE

301

SHANTI—SHANTI—SHANTI!

May there be peace in the higher regions; may there be peace in the firmament; may there be peace on earth.

May the waters flow peacefully; may the herbs and plants grow peacefully; may all the divine powers bring unto us peace. The supreme Lord is peace. May we be all in peace, peace and only peace; and may that peace come unto each of us.

Shanti (Peace)—Shanti—Shanti!

Hindu   *Vedas*

302

USELESS

Lord, let me not live to be useless.

Christian   JOHN WESLEY

303

WHERE THERE IS HATRED, LOVE

Merciful God, to Thee we commend ourselves and all those who need Thy help and correction. Where there is hatred, give love; where there is injury, pardon; where there is doubt, faith; where there is despair, hope; where there is sadness, joy; where there is darkness, light. Grant that we may not seek so much to be consoled, as to console; to be understood, as to understand; to be loved, as to love; for in giving we receive, in pardoning we are pardoned, and dying we are born into eternal life.

Christian   ST. FRANCIS

304

KNOWLEDGE

Guide us, O God the All-Knowing, to acquire knowledge. It enableth the possessor to distinguish right from wrong, it lighteth the way to heaven, it is our friend in the desert, our society in solitude, our companion when friendless; it guideth us to happiness; it sustains us in misery; it is an ornament among friends and armour against enemies.
Muslim   MUHAMMAD

305

WHETHER WE WILL OR NOT

Give us, good Lord, the will to follow whithersoever Thou leadest, but whether we will it or not follow we must.

Stoic   CLEANTHES

306

FEARFUL DOUBT

Help us to free ourselves from fearful doubt, for when we begin to doubt then doubt has no end. Thou hast no voice, O God, Thy form is unseen, yet we can hear Thy words and know Thee near.

Shinto   BUNJIRO

307

A CLEAN MIND AND A CLEAN BODY

Lord God Almighty, shaper and ruler of all creatures, we pray thee for thy great mercy to guide us to thy will, to make our minds steadfast, to strengthen us against temptation, to put far from us all unrighteousness. Shield us against our foes, seen and unseen; teach us that we may inwardly love thee before all things with a clean mind and a clean body. For thou art our Maker and our Redeemer, our help and our comfort, our trust and our hope, now and ever.

Christian   KING ALFRED

308

PRAISE BE TO GOD

In the name of the most Merciful and Compassionate God.

Praise be to God, the Lord of all creatures, the most Merciful, the Compassionate, the Master of the day of judgment. Thee alone do we worship and of Thee alone do we beg assistance. Guide us in the right way, in the way of those to whom Thou hast been gracious; not of those who have incurred wrath; nor of those who go astray.

Muslim   Opening words of *Koran,*
                              which customarily precede any prayer.

309

I WAS ANGERED

Have mercy on me O Beneficent One—I was angered for I had no shoes; then I met a man who had no feet.

Chinese

310

CREATOR OF THE UNIVERSE

O Lord Almighty, Creator of the Universe, be gracious and keep far from us all evils and let us attain whatever is beneficial to us. God, who possesses all the luminous worlds within Himself and exists from all eternity, is the only One Manifest Lord of all the created objects. He is supporting the earth and the heaven; to that All-blissful Deity we offer our humble worship.

Hindu

311

STRENGTH AND COURAGE

Father, hear the prayer we offer:
Not for ease that prayer shall be,
But for strength that we may ever
Live our lives courageously.

Christian   L. M. WILLIS

312

A GOOD CONSCIENCE

The first petition that we would make to Thee, Almighty God, is for a good conscience; the next for health of mind, and then of body.

Stoic   SENECA (adapted)

313

HELP NEEDED

Grant, O Lord, that I may be like a fire that illumines and warms, like a fountain that takes away thirst, like a tree that shelters and protects ... men are so unhappy, so ignorant, they need so much to be helped.

Hindu   SRI AUROBINDO

314

TEACH US TO SACRIFICE

O Lord, give us more charity, more self-denial, more likeness to thee. Teach us to sacrifice our comforts to others, and our likings for the sake of doing good. Make us kindly in thought, gentle in word, generous in deed. Teach us that it is better to give than to receive; better to forget ourselves than to put ourselves forward; better to minister than be ministered unto. And unto thee, the God of love, be glory and praise for ever.

Christian   HENRY ALFORD

315

GRANT ME REFUGE

I have come to Thee as a shelter. Grant me refuge, O Thou, Lord of Mercy.

Hindu   MIRA

VENTURING

. . . Thy kingdom come . . .

316

THE 'GREAT PROMISE' OF GOD

When righteousness declines and evil is strong I rise up in every age, taking visible form, and moving a man amongst men, succouring the good, thrusting the evil back, and setting virtue on her seat again.

Hindu   *Bhagavad Gita*

317

EVOLUTION!

I died as a mineral and became a plant
I died as plant and rose to animal
I died as animal and I was a man.
Why should I fear? When was I less by dying?
Yet once more I shall die as man, to soar
With angels blest; but even from angelhood
I must pass on; all except God doth perish.
When I have sacrificed my angel-soul
I shall become what no mind e'er conceived,
Oh, let me not exist! for non-existence
Proclaims in organ tones; 'To Him we shall return'.

Sufi   JELALEDDIN RUMI

318

THE LORD WILL RAISE ME UP

Even such is Time who takes in trust
    Our youth, our joys, and all we have,
And pays us but with earth and dust.
    Who, in the dark and silent grave
When we have wandered all our ways
    Shuts up the story of our days.
But from that earth, that grass, and dust,
    The Lord will raise me up, I trust.

Christian   SIR WALTER RALEIGH (written
                                                    the night before his execution)

319

PATH TO HEAVENLY BIRTH

Fearlessness, singleness of soul,
The will always to strive for wisdom;
Opened hand and governed appetites;
And piety and love of lonely study;

Humbleness, uprightness, heed to injure nought which lives,
Truthfulness, slowness unto wrath,
A mind that lightly letteth go what others prize,
And equanimity and charity which spieth no man's faults;

And tenderness towards all that suffer;
A contented heart, fluttered by no desires;
A bearing mild, modest and grave,
With manhood nobly mixed

With patience, fortitude and purity;
An unrevengeful spirit, never given to rate itself too high;
Such be the signs of him whose feet are set
On that fair path which leads to heavenly birth!

Hindu   *Bhagavad Gita*

320

NOT IN WORDS ALONE

Do not be content with showing friendship in words alone; let your heart burn with loving-kindness for all who may cross your path.

The wrong in the world continues to exist just because people talk only of their ideals, and do not strive to put them into practice. If actions took the place of words, the world's misery would very soon be changed into comfort.

Bahai   ABDU'L-BAHA

321

BECOME ONE WITH GOD

Since you have now acquired this human frame,
This is your opportunity to become one with God:
All other labours are of no use;
Seek the company of the holy and glorify God's name.

Sikh   *Rehiras* 9

322

INTELLECT CANNOT REACH

Of the kingdoms of the earth the knowledge is attainable, but the knowledge of Him with thy measure thou canst not obtain.

The bounds of His knowledge thy intellect cannot reach; nor can thy thoughts fathom the depths of His attributes. . . .

Proceed on the road of inquiry on foot, till thou reach the goal, and thence fly upwards on the pinions of affection.

But the courser of intellect can run no further. Astonishment tighteneth the reins, and exclaimeth 'Stand!'

Muslim   SADI

323

MEDITATION AND PRAYER

He who sets his heart, concentrates his mind, and sits absorbed in silent meditation shall not be a prey to evil even though living in this world of passions, and in the future world he shall receive showers of blessings ... He who with a steady heart raises his voice and without ceasing prays shall be freed from his sins and shall obtain birth into Paradise.

Buddhist   from scriptures

324

PLEASANT WATER FOR THE THIRSTY

O God, may we act with caution and wisdom; may we be truthful, hospitable, reverent; may we be a cause of healing for every sick one, a comforter for every sorrowful one, a pleasant water for every thirsty one, a table for every hungry one, a guide for every seeker, a star to every horizon, a light for every lamp, a herald for everyone yearning for Thy Kingdom.

Bahai   BAHA'U'LLAH (adapted)

325

SPLENDID USE OF OUR YEARS

O Jesus, Lord of life, we come to thee full of energies, ideals, ambitions. We would live for truth and righteousness, we would make splendid use of our years. All the future is so bright and beckoning for us. And we would bring all these things and lay them at thy feet. We would not bow down to any but thee, but before thee we must bow. We are not worthy even to be in thy presence, but we beg thee to take us as we are, and give us our orders. We will obey thee, now and for ever.

Christian   S.G.H.

326

OVERCOMING

a

May obedience overcome disobedience; peace overcome discord; liberality, avarice; humility, annoyance; a truthful speech, an untruthful utterance; the moral order, the immoral instinct.

Zoroastrian

b

Wherever we find Disorder, Thy eternal enemy, may we swiftly subdue him, make Order out of him, the subject not of Chaos but of Intelligence and of Thee. And where we find ignorance, stupidity, brute-mindedness, may we attack it and smite it in the name of God.

Christian   THOMAS CARLYLE

c

Subdue wrath by forgiveness. Overcome vanity by humbleness, fraud by straightforwardness, greed through contentment.

Jain   from scriptures

d

May we overcome anger by peacefulness; overcome evil by good; overcome the mean man by generosity, and the man who lies by truth.

Buddhist   GOTAMA

e

Be not overcome of evil, but overcome evil with good.

Christian   *Romans 12*

327

WHO SEEKS GOD FINDS HIM

Verily, verily, I say unto you that he who yearns for God finds Him.

He finds God quickest whose yearning and concentration are greatest.

Like unto a miser that longeth after gold, let thy heart pant after Him.

Men weep rivers of tears because a son is not born to them, others wear away their hearts with sorrow because they cannot get riches. But how many are there who weep and sorrow because they have not seen God. He finds who seeks Him; he who with intense longing weeps for God has found God.

Hindu   SRI RAMAKRISHNA

328

FAITH AND WORKS

Those who meditate on Thee, O God, and pronounce Thy ineffable Name, are made free; but without good works no one can find salvation.

Sikh   GURU NANAK

329

CONSCIENCE

'Shall I do this, or its reverse?'

From God comes the preference for one alternative:

'Tis from God's impulsion that man chooses one of the two . . .

Stuff not the ear of your mind with cotton,
Take the cotton of evil suggestions from the mind's ear,
That the heavenly voice from above may enter it . . .
For what is this Divine voice but the inward voice.

Sufi   JELALEDDIN RUMI

330

CAUSES, EFFECTS

From a good cause good effects must follow and from an evil cause evil effects are produced—therefore shun the evil cause. . . .

. . . If one would know past causes let him study the present effects; and if one would know future results let him know what the present causes are.

Buddhist   from scriptures

331

HONESTY IN RELIGION

O God, we worship you because you are true and eternal and unchangeable. So when we seek for Truth we know we are seeking you. Make us honest and fearless in our search. May we not be too lazy to think, and may we not be afraid if our thinking leads us into unfamiliar places. Make us really to believe what we do believe, and may we be sure that faith and honesty will in the end always bring us to you—for Jesus said 'Seek and ye shall find'.

Christian   S.G.H.

332

THE SUPREME HIGH WAY

Faith is the foundation of the Way. It cultivates every good law, removes every doubt, and it reveals and opens up the Supreme High Way. . . . It is the crown of every deed and the basis of every virtue. . . . It is the chief treasure in the treasury. . . . It is the key to understanding and knowledge.

Buddhist   from scriptures

333

TEACH US, GOOD LORD

Teach us, good Lord, to serve thee as thou deservest; to give and not to count the cost; to fight and not to heed the wounds; to toil and not to seek for rest; to labour and not to ask for any reward save that of knowing that we do thy will.

Christian   IGNATIUS LOYOLA

334

NO WEAPONS OF DESTRUCTION

The sword of a virtuous character and upright conduct is sharper than blades of steel. May we use no weapons of destruction to reshape the world. May our hosts be the hosts of goodly deeds, our arms the arms of upright conduct, and our commander Thy fear, O God.

Bahai   adapted

335

THE PIONEERS, THE BOLD ONES

God, we thank thee for the pioneers, the bold ones, who believed that man could travel on the waters, and did not rest until they had made boats; who believed that man could travel in a horseless chariot, and laboured through difficulty and scorn until an engine was built; who believed that man could fly, and persevered until at last the air was conquered; who now are preparing to explore space. We thank thee for those in the world today who believe that cancer can be banished, and poverty and war abolished, and leisure and education and comfort provided freely for all mankind. Bless those bold spirits; strengthen their hearts and their arms. Save us from ever scoffing, and may we share their faith and lend our aid towards the accomplishment of the new triumphs which thou has put into the dreams and hopes of mankind.

Christian   S.G.H.

336

HE WHO IS CALLED RIGHTEOUS

A man is not wise because he has much to say. The wise man is he who is patient, fearless and free from hatred.
A man is not wise because he knows many verses. He who knows little of the law, but lives it himself, is called righteous.

Buddhist   *Dhammapada*

337

THIS GOOD TRUTH

Then this good truth it shall be thine to know—
That oftentimes men bid their sorrows flow—
Unhappy wretches, whose slow, faltering sight
Refuse to see the blessings of the light:
And whose weak ears unconscious of a sound
List not the cheering voices waving round.

Greek   PYTHAGORAS

338

NOT IN FORCE OF ARMS

Eternal God, in whose perfect kingdom no sword is drawn but the sword of righteousness, and no strength known but the strength of love: so guide and inspire, we pray thee, the work of all who seek thy kingdom at home and abroad, that all peoples may seek and find their security, not in force of arms but in the perfect love that casteth out fear and in the fellowship revealed to us by Jesus Christ our Lord.
Christian

339

VAIN DISPUTATIONS

So long as the bee is outside the petals of the lily, and has not tasted the sweetness of its honey, it hovers round the flower emitting its buzzing sound; but when it is inside the flower it noiselessly drinks its nectar. So long as a man quarrels and disputes about doctrines and dogmas, he has not tasted the nectar of true faith; when he has tasted it, he becomes quiet and full of peace.

When water is poured into an empty vessel, a bubbling noise ensues, but when the vessel is full, no such noise is heard. Similarly, the man who has not found God is full of vain disputations about the existence and attributes of the Godhead. But he who has seen Him silently enjoys the bliss Divine.

Hindu   SRI RAMAKRISHNA

340

DISCOURSE WITH GOD

Let discourse with God be renewed every day, being preferred even to our food.

Think oftener of God than you breathe.

Stoic   EPICTETUS

341

THE GOOD MEDICINE

Wisdom is the strong ship which carries us across the sea of life and death. It is the lighthouse which lights up the encircling darkness; it is the good medicine for all patients, and the sharp axe which cuts down the trees of passions. . . . The advent of truth and wisdom is like the sunrise which drives away darkness.

Buddhist   from scriptures

342

A PRINCE AMONG MEN

He is a prince among men
Who has effaced his pride in the company of the good
He who deems himself as of the lowly
Shall be esteemed as the highest of the high.
He who lowers his mind to the dust of all men's feet,
Sees the Name of God enshrined in every heart.

Sikh   *Sukhmanu 3.* 6

343

SPACE VENTURERS

Almighty Ruler of the all
Whose power extends to great and small
Who guides the stars with steadfast law,
Whose least creation fills with awe,
Oh, grant thy mercy and thy grace
To those who venture into space.

Christian   ROBERT HEINLEIN (extra verse
for *Eternal Father Strong To Save*)

344

YIELD TO TRUTH

It is better by yielding to Truth to conquer Opinion, than by yielding
to Opinion to be defeated by Truth.
   No one is free who does not conquer himself.

Stoic   EPICTETUS

345

ADVANTAGEOUS FRIENDSHIPS

Friendship with the upright, friendship with the sincere,
      and friendship with the man of much observation:
   These three friendships are advantageous.

Confucian   *Analects 16.4*

346

THE GREATEST OF THESE IS LOVE

Through love bitter things seem sweet
Through love bits of copper are made gold
Through love pains are as healing balms
Through love thorns become roses
Through love vinegar becomes sweet wine
Through love the stake becomes a throne
Through love prison seems a rose bower

Through love hard stones become soft as butter
Through love soft wax becomes hard iron
Through love grief is as joy
Through love stings are as honey
Through love lions are harmless as mice
Through love sickness is health
Through love the dead rise to live
Through love the king becomes a slave.

Sufi   JELALEDDIN RUMI

347

AS A MOTHER

Even as a mother at the risk of her life would watch over her only child, so let us with boundless mind and goodwill survey the whole world.

Buddhist   *Metta Sutta*

348

ALL ARE BROTHERS

Perfect virtue is when you behave to everyone as if you were receiving a great guest. Within the four seas all are brothers.

Confucian

349

CITIZEN OF THE UNIVERSE

The greatest and mightiest and amplest of all societies is that which is composed of mankind and of God, and from Him have descended all creatures that are upon the earth (but especially reasoning beings, since to these alone hath nature given it to have communion and intercourse with God, being linked with Him through reason). Wherefore should such a one name himself a Citizen of the Universe, wherefore not a Son of God? Wherefore shall he fear anything that may come to pass among men? To have God for our mother and father and guardian, shall this not deliver us from griefs and fears?

Stoic   EPICTETUS

350

PUT THY TRUST IN GOD

Praise be to God and peace, and peace be on his servants. Lo, the Lord
is full of bounty for mankind. Therefore put thy trust in God.

Muslim   *Koran 27*

351

A FRIENDLY MIND

Cultivating an unbounded friendly mind,
Continually strenuous night and day,
One will spread infinite goodness through all regions.

Buddhist   *Sutta Nipata*

352

GOOD AND EVIL DEEDS

Man sees his every good deed, and says, This good deed have I done! In
no wise does he see his ill deed and say, This ill deed have I done!
Difficult, verily, is this needful self-examination. Nevertheless, a man
should see to this, knowing that these things lead to impiety, brutality,
cruelty, anger, pride, jealousy— and should say, By reason of these may
I not fall!

Buddhist   ASOKA

353

DIFFERING RELIGIOUS FORMS

A voice came from God:
To each person I have allotted peculiar forms,
To each have I given particular usages,
What is praiseworthy in thee is blameable in him . . .
In the men of Hind the usages of Hind are praiseworthy,

In the men of Sind those of Sind,
I am not purified by their praises,
'Tis they who become pure and shining thereby,
I regard not the outside and the words,
I regard the inside and the heart . . .
How long wilt thou dwell on words and superficialities?
A burning heart is what I want;
Kindle in thy heart the flame of love.
And burn up utterly thoughts and fine expressions.

Sufi   JELALEDDIN RUMI

354

NOT TO ADMIRE BUT TO FOLLOW

O Lord Jesus Christ, Thou didst not come to the world to be served, but also surely not to be admired or in that sense to be worshipped. Thou wast the way and the truth—and it was followers only Thou didst demand. Arouse us therefore if we have dozed away into this delusion, save us from the error of wishing to admire Thee instead of being willing to follow Thee and to resemble Thee.

Christian   SOREN KIERKEGAARD

355

AVERSE FROM EVIL

Lord of gentleness and love, teach us to be thy true followers: having laid aside onslaught on creatures, averse from that, may we lay aside the rod and the sword, living lives which are ashamed to hurt, endued with kindness, friendly and compassionate to all breathing living things. Having put away taking-the-not-given, averse from that, may we live lives taking and expecting only the given, with the self become pure. Having put away lying speech, averse from that, then, having put away heavy liquor and confusing drugs, may we live lives as truth-speakers, truth-thinkers, men of facts, who give reasons and do not deceive others.

Buddhist   Laymen's attestation

356

GOODNESS INCREASED

Repay injury with kindness. To those who are good to me let me be good. To those who are not good to me let me also be good. Thus shall goodness be increased.

Taoist   LAO TSE

357

MEEKNESS IS UNCONQUERABLE

Meekness is a thing unconquerable if it be true and natural, and not affected or hypocritical. For how shall even the most fierce and malicious be able to hold on against thee, if thou shalt still continue meek and loving unto him; and that even at that time when he is about to do thee wrong thou shalt be well disposed and in good temper, with all meekness to teach him and to instruct him better?

Stoic   MARCUS AURELIUS

358

ENEMIES

Men who walk in the ways of God would not grieve the hearts even of their enemies.

Muslim   SADI

359

DO GOOD

Worship and praise God, and do good unto men, bearing with them and forbearing to do them any wrong.

Stoic   MARCUS AURELIUS

360

MORAL INTEGRITY

The commander of a mighty army may be carried off into captivity, but the humblest man of his people has a will which need never be surrendered. The man of true virtue will never seek to save himself at the cost of his moral integrity, and in its defence he will be ready to sacrifice life itself.

Confucian

361

LEAD, KINDLY LIGHT

Lead, kindly Light, amid the encircling gloom
Lead Thou me on!
The night is dark, and I am far from home;
Lead Thou me on!
Keep Thou my feet; I do not ask to see
The distant scene; one step enough for me.

Christian   JOHN HENRY NEWMAN

362

JOY AND SORROW WITH EQUAL MIND

The man of Present-salvation is one
Who loves God's will with his heart and soul;
He meets joy and sorrow with an equal mind.
He is ever happy; no pain of separation for him!
To him the coveted gold is no more than dust,
And the promised nectar is no sweeter than the bitter cup of
    poison.
He is indifferent to honour and dishonour.
And makes no distinction between a prince and a pauper.
For him whatever comes from God is most reasonable;
Such a man may be said to have attained immortality while
    yet a mortal.

Sikh   *Sukhmanu 9. 7*

363

'BEATITUDES'

a

Blessed are the poor in spirit: for theirs is the
kingdom of heaven.

Blessed are they that mourn: for they shall be
comforted.

Blessed are the meek: for they shall inherit the earth.

Blessed are they which do hunger and thirst after
righteousness: for they shall be filled.

Blessed are the merciful: for they shall obtain mercy.

Blessed are the pure in heart: for they shall see God.

Blessed are the peacemakers: for they shall be called
the children of God.

Blessed are they which are persecuted for righteousness'
sake: for their's is the kingdom of heaven.

Blessed are ye, when men shall revile you, and
persecute you, and shall say all manner of evil against you
falsely, for my sake.

Rejoice and be exceeding glad: for great is your reward in
heaven: for so persecuted they the prophets which were before
you.

Christian   JESUS

b

Those who do not serve the foolish, but serve the wise;
Who honour those worthy of honour—
    They are the blessed ones.

Those with insight and education, self-control and pleasant speech;
Whose every word is well spoken—
    They are the blessed ones.

Who live righteously, giving help to kindred;
Following a peaceful calling—
    They are the blessed ones.

Who are long-suffering and meek, abhorring and ceasing from evil;
Not weary in well-doing—
    They are the blessed ones.

Who are gentle and patient under reproof;
Charitable and acting virtuously—
    They are the blessed ones.

Who are reverent and humble, content and full of gratitude;
Who are pure and temperate—
    They are the blessed ones.

Who beneath the stroke of life's changes have a mind that calm remains,
Without grief or passion—
　They are the blessed ones.

On every side they are invincible, who do acts like these,
On every side they walk in safety—
　And they are the blessed ones.

Buddhist   *Sutta Nipata* (adapted)

364

WHY WAS I BORN

In the morning when thou findest thyself unwilling to rise, consider
with thyself presently, it is to go about a man's work that I am stirred
up. Am I then yet unwilling to go about that for which I myself was
born and brought into this world? Or was I made for this, to lay me
down, and make much of myself in a warm bed?

Stoic   MARCUS AURELIUS

365

ADVENTURES IN KINDNESS

Help us, dear God, to welcome adventures in kindness. There are so
many people who need a friendly hand, who would appreciate
neighbourly aid, who are starved for sympathy and a smile, who would
be glad for the good turn that we might do. Keep us alert to see the
needs of others, may we be responsive to every true appeal for help—and
so live our lives with deep contentment according to the pattern shown
by our master, Jesus, who went about doing good.

Christian   S.G.H.

366

LOSING ALL FOR GOD

If thou desire to be even as those holy men,
Lose thy life on the way of the Friend.

Sufi   SHAIKH FARID

367

LIFE AFTER DEATH

No one understandeth save him who approacheth God,
Into whose sound heart hath entered the divine,
Who hath escaped from these narrow by-ways
To journey at large towards the sacred temple
And reposeth under the skirts of the Throne itself.

Muslim   NIZAMI

368

A MAN WITHOUT HANDS

A man without hands can receive nothing, even though he should come
to a mountain of treasure; neither can a man who has not the hands of
faith obtain anything even though he should meet the heavenly
treasures.

Buddhist   from scriptures

369

THEY WHO ARE TRUTHFUL

O Lord, it is not righteousness that we turn our faces towards the East
and the West, but righteous is the one who believes in God, and the
Last Day and the angels, and the Book, and the prophets, and gives
away wealth out of love for Him to the near of kin and the orphans and
the needy and the wayfarer and to those who ask, and sets slaves free
and keeps up prayer and pays the welfare tax; and the performers of
their promise when they make a promise, and the patient in distress and
affliction and the time of conflict. These are they who are truthful, and
these are they who keep their duty.

Muslim   *Koran 2.* 177

370

READY FOR ADVENTURE

O Jesus Christ, the Lord of all good life, who has called us to build the
city of God, do thou enrich and purify our lives, and deepen in us our
discipleship. Help us daily to know more of thee, and through us, by

the power of thy spirit, show forth thyself to other men. Make us humble, brave, and loving; make us ready for adventure in thy cause. We do not ask that thou wilt keep us safe, but that thou wilt keep us loyal: who for us didst face death unafraid, and dost live and reign for ever and ever.

Christian   *The Kingdom, the Power, and the Glory*

371
GOD IS OUR REFUGE

Turn thou to God; open thyself to God,
For He it is who possesseth, and can augment thy felicity,
In every evil let the Lord of the universe be thy refuge,
For He it is who hath power over good and evil,
He can make easy to thee every difficulty;
From Him cometh heart-cheering and victorious fortune.

Muslim   FERDUSI

372
GUIDANCE TO OUR INTELLECTS

O Thou Supreme Lord! Source of Existence, Intelligence and Bliss, Creator of the universe, may we prove worthy of thy choice and acceptance. May we meet Thy Glorious Grace. Vouchsafe unerring guidance to our intellects and may we follow Thy lead unto Righteousness.

Hindu   *Upanishads*

373
PEACE AND WAR

The best soldier is not warlike; the best fighter is never angry; the best conqueror takes no part in war.

Taoist   LAO TSE

374

A GIFT FROM THE BLESSED ONE

Forget not this, O man!
This human birth is thine—
A gift from the Blessed One.
This body is a gift to thee from God
That thou mayest in wisdom grow
And sing in thy heart the Name!

Hindu MIRA

375

GOD IN EVERYONE

May we spread ourselves abroad, O Lord, and be serviceable for Thee and Thy truth, trampling all that is contrary to God under our feet, and answering that of God in everyone.

Christian GEORGE FOX

376

FLY UNTO GOD

With all thy strength fly unto God, and surrender thyself, and by his grace thou shalt obtain Supreme Peace and reach the Eternal Home.

Hindu *Bhagavad Gita*

377

THY ONLY JOY

Let this be thy only joy, and thy only comfort—from one sociable kind action without intermission to pass unto another, God being ever in thy mind.

Stoic MARCUS AURELIUS

378

ENDING STRIFE

If one tries to end strife by strife there will be strife for ever. Forbearance alone can end strife and this is truly a precious law.... Nothing is so strong as patience; and where patience dwells malice takes flight.

Buddhist   from scriptures

379

CHANGING PEOPLE

Lord God, may I strive to make him who is our enemy, a friend; to make him who is wicked righteous; to make him who is ignorant learned.

Zoroastrian   Parsee

380

NO DISTINCTION

He excelleth who regards impartially
Lovers, friends and foes,
Strangers, neutrals, foreigners and relatives.

Hindu   *Bhagavad Gita*

WORSHIPPING AS ONE

. . . Thy will be done on earth as it is in heaven. For Thine is the kingdom and the power and the glory for ever and ever.

381

ALL PATHS ARE MINE

No matter by what path men approach me, they are made welcome. For all paths, no matter how diverse, lead straight to me. All paths are mine, notwithstanding by what names they may be called.

Hindu   *Bhagavad Gita*

382

UNTO ALL NATIONS

O God, the Creator and Preserver of all mankind, we humbly beseech thee for all sorts and conditions of men; that thou wouldest be pleased to make thy ways known unto them, thy saving health unto all nations. . . . We pray that all may be led into the way of truth and hold the faith in unity of spirit, in the bond of peace, and in righteousness of life.

Christian   *Book of Common Prayer*

383

PATHS TO GOD

The paths to God are more in number than the breathings of created beings.

Zoroastrian   Parsee

384

BROAD THE CARPET, BEAUTIFUL THE COLOURS

O God! whatever road I take joins the highway that leads to Thee.

Have the religions of mankind no common ground? Is there not everywhere the same enrapturing beauty beaming forth from many hidden places? Broad indeed is the carpet God has spread, and beautiful the colours he has given it. . . . There is but one lamp in his house, in the rays of which, wherever I look, a bright assembly meets me. . . . O God! whatever road I take joins the highway that leads to Thee.

Sufi   Abulfazl scriptures

385

AKBAR'S DREAM

Of each fair plant the choicest blooms I scan,
For of the garden of the King I'm free
To wreathe a crown for every Mussulman,
Brahmin and Buddhist, Christian and Parsee.

Shall rose cry unto lotus, 'No flower thou'?
Palm call to cypress, 'I alone am fair'?
Shall mango say to melon from his bough,
'Mine is the one fruit Allah did prepare'?

I hate the rancour of their castes and creeds,
I let men worship as their hearts commend.
I cull from every faith the noblest deeds,
And bravest soul for counsellor and friend.

And stone by stone I'll rear a sacred fane,
A temple, neither Pagod, Mosque nor Church,
Lofty and open-door'd, where all may gain
The blessing breathed by God on souls that search.

The sun shall rise at last when creed and race
Shall bear false witness each of each no more.
Before one altar Truth shall Peace embrace,
And Love and Justice kneeling shall adore.

Christian   Paraphrase of one of Tennyson's poems
                                by WILL HAYES

386

ONE AND THE SAME GOD

As with one gold various ornaments are made, having different forms
and names, so one and the same God is worshipped in different
countries and ages under different forms and names. Though He may be

worshipped in accordance with different conceptions and modes—some loving to call Him father, others mother, some calling Him friend, others calling Him the beloved, some praying to Him as the inmost treasure of their hearts, calling Him the sweet little child, yet it is one and the same God that is being worshipped in all these relations and modes.

Hindu   SRI RAMAKRISHNA

387
ALL RELIGIONS ONE

In the adorations and benedictions of righteous men
The praises of all the prophets are kneaded together
All their praises are mingled into one stream,
All the vessels are emptied into one ewer,
Because He that is praised is, in fact, only One.
In this respect all religions are only one religion,
Because all praises are directed towards God's light,
Their various forms and figures are borrowed from it.
Men never address praises but to One deemed worthy,
They err only through mistaken opinions of Him . . .
If the moon be reflected in a well,
And one looks down the well, and mistakenly praises it,
The object of his praises is the moon, not its reflection . . .
The moon is in heaven, and he fancies it in the well.

Sufi   JELALEDDIN RUMI

388
PATRIOTIC PREJUDICE

Religious, racial, political, and patriotic prejudices are the destroyers of human society. As long as these prejudices last the world of humanity will not attain to poise and perfection. As long as these threatening clouds are in the sky of humanity, the sun of reality cannot dawn.

Bahai   ABDU'L-BAHA

389

THE MOST TENDER BROTHERHOOD

To pray together, in whatever tongue or ritual, is the most tender brotherhood of hope and sympathy that men can contract in this life.

Christian   MADAME DE STAEL

390

THE ONLY TRUE MOSQUE

Fools laud and magnify the mosque,
While they strive to oppress holy men of heart,
But the former is mere form, the latter spirit and truth.
The mosque that is built in the hearts of the saints
Is the place of worship for all, for God dwells there.

Sufi   JELALEDDIN RUMI

391

A STRING OF GLEAMING PEARLS

O God, we long for the hour of love and union, the day of the spiritual harmony of all who love Thee. We strain our ears toward the East and toward the West, toward the North and toward the South, to hear the songs of love and fellowship chanted in the meetings of the faithful. We yearn to see the friends united as a string of gleaming pearls, as the brilliant Pleiades, as the rays of the sun, as the gazelles of one meadow.

May it come soon, the joyful tidings that the believers are the very embodiment of sincerity and truthfulness, the incarnation of love and amity, the living symbols of unity and concord.

Bahai   ABDU'L-BAHA

392

MONASTERY AND MOSQUE ARE THE SAME

Recognize all mankind, whether Hindus or Muslims, as one
The same Lord is the Creator and Nourisher of all:
Recognize no distinctions among them.
The monastery and the mosque are the same;
So are the Hindu worship and the Muslim prayer.
Men are all one!

Sikh   GURU GOBIND SINGH

Some seek a Father in the heavens above,
Some ask a human image to adore,
Some crave a Spirit vast as life and love;
Within thy mansions we have all and more;
Gather us in!

Christian   GEORGE MATHESON

396

IN EVERY RELIGION A SEVERAL RAY

Father of all mankind, thy people of every clime, of every creed, wait
upon thee. In thought of our common origin, all diversity is lost, and
sense of our human brotherhood alone remains. Of the one light of
Truth, teach us to see in every religion a several ray. Inspire our souls
with love of the good in every form, that we may keep our temple
always open-doored to every breath from Heaven, where Truth and
Peace may come to dwell, and prepare a way for the Universal Church,
broad as are the needs of man, and lofty as the love of God.

Zoroastrian   adapted

397

MERGING INTO GOD

As from one fire millions of sparks arise,
And though rising separately, they again unite in the fire;
As from one heap of dust, many grains of dust fill the air,
And filling it, blend with the dust again;
As in one stream, millions of waves rise up,
And being of water, sink into water again;
So, from God's form emerge
Non-sentient and sentient beings,
Who, since they arise from Him,
Shall merge into Him again.

Sikh

398

A SPIRIT OF FRIENDLINESS

Consort with the followers of all religions in a spirit of friendliness and
fellowship.

Bahai   BAHA'U'LLAH

399

MADE OF ONE BLOOD

One is your Father and all ye are brethren. . . . God is no respecter of persons, but in every nation he that feareth him and worketh righteousness is accepted with him. . . . He hath made of one blood all nations of the earth.

Christian   *New Testament*

400

GREAT SOULS AND GREAT HOUSES

You will confer the greatest Benefits on your City, not by raising the Roofs, but by exalting the Souls. For it is better that great Souls should live in small Habitations, than that abject Slaves should burrow in great Houses.

Stoic   EPICTETUS

401

LET US BE UNITED

O God,
Let us be united;
Let us speak in harmony;
Let our minds apprehend alike.
Common be our prayer;
Common be the end of our assembly;
Common be our resolution;
Common be our deliberations.
Alike be our feelings;
Unified be our hearts;
Common be our intentions;
Perfect be our unity.

Hindu   *Rig Veda*

402

ALL PEOPLE

May we who follow the light of love, associate with all people of the
world, with men of all religions, in concord and harmony; in the spirit
of perfect joy and fragrance. Let not thy Word, O God, be made a cause
of opposition and stumbling, or the cause of hatred among men. If we
have a word or an essence which another has not, may we say it to him
with the tongue of love and kindness, for the tongue of kindness is
attractive to the heart and is the sword of the spirit. We creatures were
created through love; let us live in peace and amity.

Bahai   BAHA'U'LLAH (adapted)

403

PEACE–PEACE–PEACE

Om* ...
May God protect us,
May he guide us,
May he give us strength and right understanding,
May love and harmony be with us all,
Om ... Peace–Peace–Peace.

Hindu   *Upanishads*

*(Om, see 33)

404

THE CHURCH UNIVERSAL

One holy Church of God appears
Through every age and race,
Unwasted by the lapse of years,
Unchanged by changing place.

From oldest time, on farthest shores,
Beneath the pine or palm,
One unseen presence she adores,
With silence or with psalm.

Her priests are all God's faithful sons
To serve the world raised up;
The pure in heart her baptized ones,
Love, her communion cup.

The truth is her prophetic gift,
The soul her sacred page;
And feet on mercy's errand swift
Do make her pilgrimage.

O living Church, thine errand speed;
Fulfil thy task sublime;
With bread of life earth's hunger feed;
Redeem the evil time!

Christian   SAMUEL LONGFELLOW

405

LET THY LIGHT FALL

O Divine Master, let Thy light fall upon this chaos and a new world emerge from it. What is now preparing accomplish and let a new humanity be born which will be the perfect expression of thy sublime Law.

Salutation to Thee, O Master of the worlds, who triumphest over every obscurity.

Hindu   SRI AUROBINDO

406

THIS WORLD AND THE OTHER WORLD

Beneficent God, may cheerfulness, joy and goodness arrive to men; may disease, misery, selfishness and all such evil fly away. May the good be powerful. May the evil-minded be powerless and may they repent of their evil deeds. May our thoughts, words and actions be on the line of righteousness. We pray for the good of the life of all living creatures which Thou hast created. May the faith which worships one omniscient God spread and continue in the wide world. May the thoughts, words and actions of us all be truthful and righteous, so that, in the end, all mankind may be benefited in this world and in the other world.

Zoroastrian

407

GROWING TOGETHER

A branch is cut off from the whole tree by another, but he that hates cuts himself off from his neighbour, and knows not that at the same time he divides himself from the whole body or corporation. But herein is the gift and mercy of God, the Author of this society, in that once cut off we may grow together and become part of the whole again.

Stoic   MARCUS AURELIUS

408

MANKIND A SINGLE NATION

O God it is thy word that mankind is a single nation, so all human beings are born free and equal in dignity and rights, they are endowed with reason and conscience and should act towards one another in a spirit of brotherhood.

Muslim   *Koran,* and *United Nations Universal Declaration of Human Rights*

409

DIFFERENT CREEDS ARE DIFFERENT PATHS

Different creeds are but different paths to reach the Almighty. Various and different are the ways that lead to the temple of Mother Kali at Kalighat (near Calcutta). Similarly, various are the ways that lead to the house of the Lord. Every religion is nothing but one of such paths that lead to God.

Hindu   SRI RAMAKRISHNA

410

THIS FRATERNAL GATHERING

Eternal and Almighty God, look favourably upon this our fraternal gathering so that each one of us, overcoming and repudiating our differences and the adversities which poison human relations, will spread all around us the seeds of goodness and become messengers of love and life. Only with thy help, O provident Creator, will the impetus of our concord be able to break down the barriers of egoism and misunderstanding.

Christian   (A prayer by Cardinal Bea at a gathering
                                    of Protestants, Jews, Muslims, Buddhists, 1962)

411

ALL MEN BROTHERS

Lord God the Almighty, may all the nations become one in faith and all men be brothers; may the bonds of affection and unity be strengthened; may diversity of religion cease and differences of race be annulled. May fruitless strife and ruinous wars pass away and the Most Great Peace come. Let not man glory in this, that he loves his country; let him rather glory in this, that he loves his kind.

Bahai   adapted

412

UNITY OF THE RIGHTEOUS

God, Ruler of all, may we be all one in co-operation with righteous men throughout the whole world. May we be one with them and may they be one with us. May we all benefit one another and help one another.

Zoroastrian

413

ACCORDING TO HIS ACTS

I call heaven and earth to witness that whether a person be Jew or Gentile, man or woman, manservant or maidservant, according to his acts does the Divine Spirit rest upon him.

Jewish   *Seder Eliyahu Rabbah*

414

EVERY RELIGION SHOWS ONE WAY

As one can ascend to the top of a house by means of a ladder or a bamboo or a staircase or a rope, so divers are the ways and means to approach God, and every religion in the world shows one of these ways.

Hindu SRI RAMAKRISHNA

415

GOD, THE DIVINE GURU

One man by shaving his head is accepted as a Sanyasi,
Another as a Jogi or a Brahmachari, a third as a Jati.
Some are Hindus and others Moslems;
Of these, some are Rafazis, Imams and Shafais—
Understand that all men are of the same caste.
Kartar and Karim are the same;
Razak and Rahim are the same;
Let none, even mistakenly, suppose there is a difference.
Worship the one God who is the one divine Guru for all;
Know that His Form is one,
And that He is the one light diffused in all.

Sikh GURU GOBIND SINGH

416

MAKING A BETTER WORLD

O thou invisible Maker and Ruler of all the earth, who dost put down the mighty from their seats and exalt the humble and meek, aid us in making an end of tyranny and injustice in every land. Raise up men of mercy and goodwill who, seeking nothing for self, may hasten justice, happiness and peace among men.

Christian S.G.H.

417

ALL MANKIND

We pray for all mankind. Though divided into nations and races, yet we all are Thy children, drawing from Thee our life and being. Cause hatred and strife to vanish, that abiding peace may fill the earth, and all men may be blessed. So shall the spirit of brotherhood among men show forth their faith that Thou art the Father of all.

Jewish *Liberal Prayer Book*

418

DIFFERENT PATHS FOR DIFFERENT MEN

People partition off their lands by means of boundaries, but no one can partition off the all-embracing sky overhead. The indivisible sky surrounds all and includes all. So, a man in ignorance says: 'My religion is the only one, my religion is the best.' But when his heart is illumined by true knowledge, he knows that above all these wars of sects and sectarians presides the one indivisible, eternal, all-knowing bliss.

As a mother, in nursing her sick children, gives rice and curry to one, and sago and arrowroot to another and bread and butter to a third, so the Lord has laid out different paths for different men suitable to their natures.

Hindu   SRI RAMAKRISHNA

419

THE RELIGION OF LOVE

My heart is capable of every form; it is a pasture for gazelles and a convent for Christian monks, the pilgrim's Kaaba, the tables of the *Torah* and the book of the *Koran.* I follow the religion of Love, whichever way his camels take.

Sufi

420

ALL BROTHERS AND SISTERS

May the time be not distant, O God, when all your children will understand that they are brothers and sisters, so that, one in spirit and one in fellowship, they may be for ever united before you. Then shall your kingdom be established on earth, and the word of your prophet shall be fulfilled: 'The Lord will reign for ever and ever.'

Jewish   *Service of the Heart*

421

A VISION OF OUR LAND

O God, grant us a vision of our land, fair as she might be; a land of justice, where none shall prey on others; a land of plenty, where vice and poverty shall cease to fester; a land of brotherhood, where all success shall be founded on service, and honour shall be given to nobleness alone; a land of peace, where order shall not rest on force, but on the love of all for the land, the great mother of the common life and weal. Hear thou, O Lord, the silent prayer of all our hearts, as we pledge our time and strength and thought to speed the day of her coming beauty and righteousness.

Christian   WALTER RAUSCHENBUSCH

422

MAKE THE NATIONS ONE

O Thou kind Lord! Thou hast created all humanity from the same stock. Thou hast decreed that all shall belong to the same household. In Thy Holy Presence they are all Thy servants, and all mankind are sheltered beneath Thy Tabernacle; all have gathered together at Thy Table of Bounty: all are illumined through the light of Thy Providence.

O Thou kind Lord! Unite all. Let the religions agree and make the nations one, so that they may see each other as one family and the whole earth as one home. May they all live together in perfect harmony.

O God! Raise aloft the banner of the oneness of mankind.

Bahai   ABDU'L-BAHA

423

MAN'S BROTHERHOOD

You are forgetting, too, the closeness of man's brotherhood with his kind; a brotherhood not of blood or human seed, but of a common intelligence; and that this intelligence in every man is God, an emanation from the deity.

Men exist for each other. Then either improve them or put up with them.

Stoic   MARCUS AURELIUS

424

SKIN TINTS

Thank you, God, that your various earth children are so fascinatingly diverse; that some of us have pink skins, and our brothers in other climes are brown or yellow, or black or red. Forgive us that we have often childishly and quarrelsomely claimed one colour to be superior to another, and grant that we may strive to make humanity as single and whole and variedly beautiful as your multi-coloured rainbow.

Christian   S.G.H.

425

THE DEVOTEE

Whatever form a devotee seeks
I stabilize his faith that makes
Him to realize the vision
Which removes all confusion.

He who sees Me present in all
And all in me, Universal Soul,
I am never out of sight of him
Nor is he out of my wisdom.

Whosoever offers a leaf or flower
With love, a fruit or even water,
In person I shall appear before him
And partake that offered with love supreme.

Hindu   *Bhagavad Gita*

426

THE CORD OF GOD

Hold ye fast the cord of God, all of you;
    and break not loose from it. Remember God's goodness towards you.
He united your hearts;
    and by His favour ye became brethren.

Muslim   *Koran 3.* 103

427

IN THE HEARTS OF ALL

God is seated in the hearts of all.

Hindu   *Bhagavad Gita*

428

THE FAMILY OF GOD

All thy creatures, O God, form Thy family, and he is the best loved of
Thee who loveth best Thy creatures. O Lord, Lord of my life and of
everything in the universe, I affirm that all human beings are brothers
unto one another, so may we respect Thy ways and be affectionate to
the Family of God.

Muslim

429

THE HOLY BAND

He, the Lord of all
Never doth ask thee
What is thy caste!
He who sings of Him
And serves His creatures
He belongs to the Holy Band
Of His worshippers indeed!

Hindu   RAIDAS

430

MEN OF ALL SECTS

The Beloved of the Gods honours men of all sects with gift and
manifold honour. But the Beloved of the Gods does not think so much
of gift and honour as that there should be a growth of the essential
among men of all sects. . . .

   Coming together of the sects is therefore commendable in order that
they may hear and desire to hear one another's teaching. For this is the
desire of the Beloved of the Gods, that all sects shall be well informed
and conducive of good.

And those who are favourably disposed towards this or that sect shall be informed: The Beloved of the Gods does not so much think of gift or honour as that there may be a growth of the essential among all sects and also mutual appreciation.

Buddhist   ASOKA

431

THE REIGN OF PEACE

O Lord, O inconceivable Splendour, may thy Beauty overflow the earth, may thy Love be kindled in all hearts and the reign of thy Peace be upon all.

Hindu   SRI AUROBINDO

432

THE SHINING CITY OF GOD

O Christ, thou hast bidden us pray for the coming of thy Father's Kingdom in which righteousness will be done on earth. We have treasured thy words, but we have forgotten their meaning, and thy great hope has grown dim in thy church. We bless thee for the inspired souls of all ages who saw afar the shining city of God. As we have mastered nature that we might gain wealth, help us now to master the social relations of mankind that we may gain justice and a world of brothers.

Make us determined to live by truth and not by lies, to found our common life on the eternal foundations of righteousness and love, and no longer to prop the tottering house of wrong by legalized cruelty and force. Help us to make the welfare of all the supreme law of our land, that so our commonwealth may be built strong and secure on the love of all its citizens. Our Master, once more we make thy faith our prayer: 'Thy kingdom come. Thy will be done on earth.' Amen

Christian   WALTER RAUSCHENBUSCH

433

THE LIGHT OF UNITY

God grant that the light of unity may envelop the whole earth, and that the seal, 'the Kingdom is God's', may be stamped upon the brow of all its peoples.

Bahai   BAHA'U'LLAH

434

WELFARE AND HAPPINESS

Among people of all denominations the promoting and establishment of piety must be encouraged, and the increase of the welfare and happiness of all people—the rich, the poor, the aged, the servants and the masters.

Buddhist   ASOKA

435

WORSHIP IS ONE

Altar flowers are of many species, but all worship is one. Systems of Faith are different, but God is one.

Hindu

436

EACH QUARTER OF THE WORLD

Thy true servant lets his mind pervade one quarter of the world with thoughts of Love, with thoughts of Compassion, with thoughts of understanding Joy and with thoughts of Equanimity; and so the second quarter, and so the third, and so the fourth. And thus the whole wide world, above, below, around, and everywhere, does he continue to pervade with heart of Love, Compassion, Joy and Equanimity, far-reaching, great, beyond measure, free from the least trace of anger or ill-will.

Buddhist   *Maha-Sudassana Sutta*

437

TEMPLES SHALL RISE AND PRAISE BE SUNG

O Thou, to whom in ancient time the lyre of Hebrew bards was strung, whom kings adored in song sublime, and prophets praised with glowing tongue!

From every place below the skies the grateful song, the fervent prayer, the incense of the heart may rise to Heaven and find acceptance there.

To Thee shall age with snowy hair, and strength and beauty bend the knee; and childhood lisp with reverent air its praises and its prayers to thee.

O Thou, to whom in ancient time the lyre of prophet bards was strung, to Thee at last in every clime shall temples rise and praise be sung.

Christian   JOHN PIERPONT

438

THE GRANDEUR OF TRUTH

What words can sing thy ineffable Peace and celebrate the Majesty of thy Silence and the Grandeur of thy omnipotent Truth!

The whole manifested world cannot speak thy splendour and recount thy marvels, and in the eternity of time it is this which it has been trying to do more and more, better and better, eternally.

Hindu   SRI AUROBINDO

439

ALL THINGS ONE

For all things throughout there is but one and the same order, and through all things one and the same God, the same substance and the same Lord. There is one common reason, and one common truth, that belongs unto all reasonable creatures, for neither is there save one perfection of all creatures that are of the same kind, and partakers of the same reason.

Stoic   MARCUS AURELIUS

440

TRUE RELIGION

a

All true religion consists of obedience to thy will as Sovereign of the world, in confidence in thy declarations, and in imitation of thy perfection.

Christian   EDMUND BURKE (adapted)

b

Religion does not consist in subscribing to this creed or that creed, but in coming face to face with Thee.

Hindu   *Vedas*

c

Pure religion and undefiled before God and the Father is this, to visit the fatherless and the widows in their affliction, and to keep oneself unspotted from the world.

Christian   *James 1*

d

Not he that saith Lord, Lord, but he that doeth the will of my Father which is in heaven.

Christian   JESUS

e

Just Words do not the saint or sinner make, Action alone is written in the book of fate.

Sikh   *Japji* 20

f

True religion is to love, as God has loved, all things both great and small.

Hindu   *Hitopadesa*

g

Be done with self and worship Hari (God); cast off worldly desire in mind and body.

Cherish goodwill towards every living creature.

This is the sum of religion.

Hindu   DADU

441

EXPLORING WHAT UNITES

O God, give to all those in the world who seek thee a new understanding of their oneness, that, forgetting what divides, they may so explore what unites that the whole world may at, last become one family, in love and forbearance and a common joy.

Christian   S.G.H.

442

LIT FROM THE SAME LIGHT

O Thou who art the Kernel of Existence, reconcile us all into love of each other and of Thee, for all lamps are lit from the same Light.

Sufi   JELALEDDIN RUMI (adapted)

443

TRUTH IS ONE

Truth is one: sages call it through various names.
It is the one Sun who reflects in all the ponds;
It is the one water which slakes the thirst of all;
It is the one air which sustains all life;
It is the one fire which shines in all houses;
Colours of the cows may be different, but milk
is white; Flowers and bees may be different, but
honey is the same; Systems of faiths may be
different, but God is one.

As the rain dropping from the sky
wends its way towards the ocean,
So the prostrations offered in all faiths reach the One
God, who is supreme.

Hindu   *Rig Veda*

444

ONE BROTHERHOOD FOR EVERMORE

Great God, unite our severing ways;
No separate altars may we raise,
But with one tongue now speak thy praise—

With peace that comes of purity
Building the temple yet to be,
To fold our broad humanity.

White flowers of love its walls shall climb,
Soft bells of peace shall ring its chime,
Its days shall all be holy time.

A sweeter song shall then be heard—
The music of the world's accord,
Rejoicing o'er the broken sword.

That song shall swell from shore to shore
One hope, one faith, one love restore,
One brotherhood for evermore.

Christian   JOHN GREENLEAF WHITTIER

445

THE SAME WAGON-POLE

Let us come together to the glory of the mighty Guardian; may our minds and purposes be united. May we be in harmony with our kinsfolk, in harmony with strangers. Like friends may we associate, devoted to the same purpose, speaking words in kindly spirit, not holding ourselves apart, co-operating, going along the same wagon-pole, speaking agreeably to one another.

Hindu   *Atharva Vedas* (adapted)

APPENDIX

An interesting thought

Does the great spiritual leader, or event, or the resurgence of religion in some new form, happen at recognisable periods in human history? Can such fresh emergings of spiritual consciousness be in any way anticipated? Is the next one due around the year 2500?—It is at least an interesting thought.

Here is a speculative tabulation of major religious happenings and personalities of world significance. It suggests that each 500 years there is a rebirth of cosmic understanding and awakened faith. Obviously the dates given are only approximate—Maimonides 1000 for example, and Islam 500—but they are at least sufficiently near to form a basis for stimulating discussion and investigation.

Approximate dates

2000	B.C.	Abraham
1500		Akhnaton
		Vedas
1000		Zoroaster
500		Gotama
		Confucius
		Socrates
		Lao Tse
		Mahavira
1	A.D.	Jesus
500		Islam
1000		Maimonides

1500   Luther reforms Christianity
              Guru Nanak reforms Hinduism
              Sikhism founded

2000   Gandhi
              Bahai faith founded
              Zen Buddhist expansion

I think it is true that no names or events of comparable significance have been omitted.

S.G.H.

TITLE INDEX

(References are to the numbered items)

SOURCE INDEX

(References are to the numbered items)

BUDDHA (see GOTAMA)
BUNJIRO, Shinto reformer, began as priest, but taught a monotheistic, homely form of worship (1814-83): 189, 222, 299, 306
BURKE, EDMUND (1729-97): 440a

CARLYLE, THOMAS (1795-1881): 326b
CARMICHAEL, AMY WILSON: 97
CASARTELLI, L.C.: 245
Chinese, Prayers of Chinese Emperor of Ming Dynasty (1538): 10, 204
Christian Epigrams: 292
CLEANTHES, Stoic philosopher, disciple of Zeno: 35 (from *The Hymn of Cleanthes*, trs. Gilbert West): 61, 305
CONFUCIUS, Chinese sage and philosopher (*c.*551-479 B.C.). No. 345 from his *Analects*

DADU, poet, seer, mystic; successor of Kabir and Raides; founder of Hindu sect in 16th century A.D. at centre of whose worship was repetition of God's name, Rama. Modern Western meditation cults often use same technique, repeating the 'mantra' Ram: 17, 33, 227l, 261r, 440g
Dhammapada, Buddhist scripture or 'hymnbook': 69, 163, 336
DODDRIDGE, PHILIP (1702-51): 300
DONNE, JOHN (1573-1631): 244
DOWDEN, EDWARD, 19th century Irish critic and poet: 118

Eastern Church: 250b
Ecclesiasticus: 1
ELLERTON, JOHN (1826-93): 228b
ELMSLIE, W. GRAY (1848-89): 43
EPICTETUS, Stoic philosopher of 1st century. He was lame, and lived a slave in Rome. It was said of him: 'A slave, a cripple, Epictetus trod this earth in penury—the Friend of God': 67, 85, 133, 136, 143, 171, 185, 201, 265, 340, 344, 349, 400

FARID, SHAIKH, Indian Sufi (15th century): 366
FENELON, French prelate and writer (1651-1715): 274
FERDUSI, Muslim Persian poet (10th century): 44, 49, 152, and 371 (trs. by S. Robinson)
FOWLER, ELLEN THORNEYCROFT: 264
FOX, GEORGE, founder of the Society of Friends (Quakers) (1624-90): 295, 375
FRANCIS, ST. (1182-1226): 52, 202, 303

GAUTAMA (see GOTAMA)
Gelasian Sacramentary, having to do with Gelasius I, pope from 492 to 496: 227c
GERHARDT, PAULUS (1607-76): 190

Gita (see *Bhagavad Gita*)

GOBIND SINGH, last of the ten Sikh prophets or Gurus (1666-1708):
47, 55, 131, 228a, 270, 392, 415

Gospel of Zarathustra: 64f

GOTAMA (or Gautama; the BUDDHA), founder of Buddhism (5th
century B.C.). He left disciples who, like Christ's, set out to
preach their gospel to all: 75, 326d

Granth, The, Sikh scripture: 119

Greek Church liturgy: 227a

HAVERGAL, FRANCES R. (1836-79): 230b

HAYES, WILL: 385

HEINLEIN, ROBERT: 343

HICKSON, W.E. (1803-70): 231c

HILLEL, born in Babylon *c.* 112 B.C., notable Jewish rabbi. Died, it is
said, at age of 120: 64g

Hitopadesa, Hindu scripture, a book of wisdom or good counsel: 440f

HONEN SHONIN, saintly Buddhist leader (1133-1212): 99

HOYLAND, JOHN S., Quaker poet (1830-94): 31, 38, 176, 186,
210, 221

HUNTER, JOHN: 74, 246, 255, 281

Hymns and prayers for Dragons: 93, from Dragon School, Oxford.

IBN ATA ALLAH, Sufi of Alexandria: 285 (from *Sufism* by
A. J. Arberry)

Indian College prayer: 62

Inner Light: 231b

Jain (pronounced *jine*) scriptures, *c.* 500 B.C. Jains, vegetarian
pacifists, respect all life, teaching self-reliance and the
individuality and indestructability of the human soul: 154, 261j,
326c.

JAMI, 15th century Persian Muslim poet,: 140, 159, 216, 286, (trs. S.
Robinson)

Japji, No. 3 is the *Mool Mantra* (opening verse) of this Sikh scripture
and usually precedes most other prayers: 115, 440e

JELALEDDIN RUMI, Persian Sufi mystic and poet, the 'Milton or
Dante of Muslims', (15th century). Founded an Order of
Dervishes in whose convents the Whirling Dance was a distinctive
ritual: 103, 267, 293, 317, 329, 346, 353, 387, 390, 442, (trs.
E.H. Whinfield; 293 by R.A. Nicholson)

JESUS (CHRIST) (1-33 A.D.): 64a, 363a, 440d

JOHN OF THE CROSS, ST. (16th century): 110

KABIR, 15th century Indian saint who declared that all religion
had truth and God could be called Allah by Muslims or Rama
or Krishna by Hindus—both faiths claimed him at his death.
He influenced Nanak who founded Sikhism. Kabir's followers
resembled Quakers: 37, 145, 150, 227k

GROUPINGS BY FAITHS

BAHAI

5, 18, 28, 71, 79, 84, 106, 113, 120, 151, 196, 211, 234a, 261q,
283, 320, 324, 334, 388, 391, 394, 398, 402, 411, 422, 433

BUDDHIST

64b, 69, 75, 77, 83, 87, 89, 92, 94, 99, 111, 116, 142, 148, 153,
158, 163, 167, 182, 227g, 235, 261h, 261k, 269, 323, 326d, 330, 332,
336, 341, 347, 351, 352, 355, 363b, 368, 378, 430, 434, 436

CHINESE

10, 89, 204, 309

CHRISTIAN

2, 13, 21, 23, 27, 31, 38, 43, 48, 52, 62, 64a, 70, 74, 82, 86,
88, 90, 93, 96, 97, 100, 102, 104, 110, 118, 123, 127, 130, 135, 144,
149, 156, 160, 166, 170, 172, 176, 181, 186, 190, 194, 199, 202, 210,
214, 221, 227a, 227c, 227e, 228b, 229a, 229c, 230a, 230b, 231a, 231b,
231c, 232a, 232c, 234b, 234c, 236, 237, 238, 239, 240, 241, 242b,
242d, 242f, 242h, 244, 246, 247, 249, 250a, 250c, 251, 253, 255,
257, 258, 260b, 260d, 261f, 261o, 263, 264, 266, 268, 271, 274,
277, 279, 281, 287, 289, 292, 295, 297, 300, 302, 303, 307, 311,
314, 318, 325, 326b, 326e, 331, 333, 335, 338, 343, 354, 361, 363a,
365, 370, 375, 382, 385, 389, 393, 395, 399, 404, 410, 416, 421,
424, 432, 437, 440a, 440c, 440d, 441, 444

CONFUCIAN

64c, 72, 121, 125, 227d, 345, 348, 360

EGYPTIAN

9, 15, 32, 39, 45, 56, 132, 208, 219

GREEK

147, 243, 337

HINDU

7, 14, 17, 22, 33, 42, 46, 50, 58, 60, 66, 73, 76, 81, 98, 107, 112, 117, 124, 128, 134, 139, 155, 161, 165, 173, 179, 183, 191, 193, 197, 200, 203, 205, 207, 209, 212, 215, 218, 224, 227b, 227i,l, 229b, 230c, 232b, 242a, 242c, 242e, 259, 260f, 261e,m,r, 272, 275, 280, 290, 296, 298, 301, 310, 313, 315, 316, 319, 327, 339, 372, 374, 376, 380, 381, 386, 401, 403, 405, 409, 414, 418, 425, 527, 429, 431, 435, 438, 440b,g, 440f, 443, 445

JAIN

154, 261j, 326c

JEWISH

1, 6, 41, 51, 53, 57, 59, 63, 64g, 138, 192, 198, 233, 252, 254, 260h, 261d, 262, 291, 413, 417, 420

MANICHAEAN

178, 294

MUSLIM

4, 16, 19, 25, 30, 36, 40, 44, 49, 54, 64d, 68, 80, 91, 103, 126, 140, 152, 159, 174, 206, 213, 216, 220, 223, 225, 227f, 227h, 229d, 242g, 248, 260a, 261b, 261l, 273, 276, 286, 304, 308, 317, 322, 350, 358, 367, 369, 371, 408, 426, 428

SHINTO

189, 222, 261i, 282, 299, 306

SIKH

3, 11, 17, 26, 34, 37, 47, 55, 78, 101, 109, 115, 119, 131, 141, 146, 150, 164, 180, 184, 187, 195, 226, 228a, 260e, 261g, 261n, 270, 278, 321, 328, 342, 362, 366, 392, 397, 415, 440e

STOIC

35, 67, 85, 95, 114, 133, 136, 143, 157, 162, 171, 185, 201, 217, 256, 265, 305, 312, 340, 344, 349, 357, 359, 364, 377, 400, 407, 423, 439

SUFI

12, 64e, 105, 129, 137, 169, 177, 261p, 267, 285, 293, 317, 329, 346, 353, 384, 387, 390, 419, 442

ACKNOWLEDGMENTS

MY sincere thanks are due to the following authors and owners of copyrights for permitting me to use prayers and extracts from their writings or books:

Y.M.C.A., *A Book of Prayers*, for No. 166; Macmillan & Co. Ltd., with Mrs. Iris Wise for No. 2, and with the Trustees of the Tagore Estate for Nos. 134, 242; Routledge and Kegan Paul, *Liberal Jewish Prayer Book*; Miss S. Wadia, *The Message of Zoroaster*; University of Chicago Press, *The Prayers of Kierkegaard*; The Headmaster, Dragon School, Oxford; Church of Scotland Youth Department, *A Pattern of Prayer* by A.W. Sawyer; Ashram Pondicherry, *Prayers and Meditations of the Mother* by Sri Aurobindo; Egyptian Exploration Society; W. Heffer & Sons Ltd., *Silent Dawn* by John S. Hoyland; Ramakrishna Vedanta, Calcutta, *The Sayings of Ramakrishna*; C.S. Lewis; Pilgrim Press, Massachusetts—Walter Rauschenbusch; Dr. Leslie Hunter—John Hunter; Luzac & Co., *The Udana*; Bahai Publishing Trust; John Murray Ltd., *Invocations of Ansari* by Sir Jogendra Singh (Wisdom of the East Series), Nos. 12, 64e, 105, 129, 169, 177, 261p; George Allen & Unwin Ltd., *Rumi, Poet and Mystic*, trs. R.A. Nicholson, No. 293; Laurence Pollinger Ltd., *The Green Hills of the North*, Robert Heinlein, No. 343; Union of Liberal and Progressive Synagogues *Service of the Heart*, Nos. 6, 198, 420.

The quotation from *The Book of Common Prayer* is included by permission; also the text of the Authorized Version of the Bible is Crown Copyright and extracts herein are reproduced by permission.

I have made every effort to discover the owner of each copyright, but if, inadvertently, I have overlooked any proper acknowledgments, I trust I may be forgiven, and will gladly make the necessary correction in any later edition.

S.G.H.